RE-SEARCHING BLACK MUSIC

ALSO BY THE AUTHOR

As the Black School Sings (1987)
Sacred Symphony (1987)
Protest and Praise (1990)
Theological Music (1991)
Black Hymnody (1992)
Blues and Evil (1993)
The Rhythms of Black Folk (1995)
Sing a New Song (1995)

RE-SEARCHING BLACK MUSIC

Jon Michael Spencer

The University of Tennessee Press / Knoxville

Copyright © 1996 by The University of Tennessee Press / Knoxville.
All Rights Reserved.
Cloth: 1st printing, 1996.
Paper: 1st printing, 2017.

Library of Congress Cataloging-in-Publication Data

Spencer, Jon Michael.
  Re-searching Black music / Jon Michael Spencer. — 1st ed.
    p. cm.
  Includes bibliographical references and index.
  ISBN-13 978-1-62190-305-5
  1. Afro-Americans—Music—History and criticism.
  2. Music—United States—History and criticism. I. Title.
ML3556.S83 1996
780'.89' 96073—dc20   95-41760
                                                          CIP
                                                          MN

For Eileen Southern

CONTENTS

	Foreword	ix
	Prologue	xiii
	Introduction	1
1.	The Rhythm	11
2.	The Religion	30
3.	Folk Muse	47
4.	Popular Muse	65
5.	Classical Muse	89
6.	An Ethics	107
	Conclusion	129
	Notes	135
	Select Bibliography	147
	Index	151

FOREWORD

The following prologue is an important part of this book, and its importance will unfold as I make reference to its relationship to the re-search of black music in each of the chapters. I will not say anything about that relationship at this time, for I must present my case carefully and incrementally—starting with the prologue itself.

What I do want to say briefly is that the following prologue is my best effort at what blues singers Robert Johnson, Son House, Bessie Smith, and Big Bill Broonzy meant by "preaching the blues" in their songs of that title. Had church folk during their day not considered them evil—singers of devil's music—and had church folk permitted them to preach their down-to-earth messages in church, then perhaps these blues singers would have uttered words of ethicality similar to those of my prologue, which I preached at a small black Episcopal church in Greenwood, Mississippi.[1] It was Sunday, September 19, 1993, the morning after the Sixteenth Annual Mississippi Delta Blues Festival. I had been in Greenwood to speak at a symposium on the religious nature of the blues, but the person who organized the symposium was the pastor of this church (Church of the Redeemer) and he asked me to preach in addition.

I accepted the invitation to preach, as any bluesman would, knowing that this was my opportunity to justify the blues as had so many blues people before me. Henry Townsend had said, "Some people think that the blues is something that is evil—I don't. If the blues is delivered in the truth, which most of them are, . . . if I sing the blues and tell the truth, what have I done? What have I committed? I haven't lied."[2] Blues singer Willie Thomas, believing blues to be in no way contradictory to the nature of God, contended that when church folk sing "Lord, have mercy, save poor me," they are actually singing the blues.[3] Similarly, John Lee Hooker concluded that when the spirituals were created they were created "on the blues side," their kinship being the reason he decided to quit singing the spirituals and start singing the blues.[4] Compelled to preach the blues like Johnson, House, Smith, and Broonzy, and to justify the blues like Townsend, Thomas, and Hooker, I decided it would be only fitting that I should write my sermon for the small Greenwood church while immersing myself in the blues at the Delta festival. I also thought it would be appropriate to write my sermon this way since I would be preaching not as a Christian minister but as a scholar interested in re-searching black music.

But how does a scholar interested in re-searching black music arrive at the point where he can not only preach in church but preach the blues—not as a blues singer but as a musicologist? In the course of this book I will argue that the ethics that my sermon espouses and the ethical praxis of my preaching it are natural consequences of re-searching black music—*re*-searching it because of the evident fact that worlds of knowledge have been neglected in past scholarship. The sermon follows in the prologue.

Before I get to that, however, I would like to thank Meredith Morris-Babb of the University of Tennessee Press for working with me on this book when it was in manuscript form and for her encouragement that certain revisions suggested by the readers could make this a better work. I am equally grateful to two of the three readers who identified themselves—Lawrence Mamiya of Vassar College and Katrina Hazzard-Gordon of Rutgers University. Their remarks helped me to rethink and improve on certain sections of the book. And for seeing the book to fruition I thank Stan Ivester, the managing editor of the University of Tennessee Press.

PROLOGUE

Whither shall I go from thy spirit?
or whither shall I flee from thy presence?
If I ascend up into heaven, thou art there:
if I make my bed in hell, behold, thou art there.
   —Psalm 139:7-8 (King James Version)

It is the foregoing text that strikes me as being appropriate to contextualize biblically my theological apology for the blues in this sermon, an apology that results from my sense of certainty that blues are no more "evil" than the biblical psalms or lamentations. There are people, however, who seem to look to the blues in order to get in touch with the evil that is really in themselves, evil in themselves that is denied because of their impermissible religious doctrine. These people then project the suppressed evil in themselves onto the blues and onto those who sing and listen to the blues, and they call the blues "devil's music" and label blues singers "Satan's musicians."

Perhaps it is true that the men and women who left the church to sing the blues were not forced to leave that holy sanctuary where God was. Perhaps they did not have to quit that place of spiritual and social refuge which periodically shielded them from the hostile world—plantation peonage, rampant lynching, political disfranchisement, and unequal social and economic status. They could have remained in the church and escaped to that "heaven" as frequently as the rest of the community—escaped to prayer meetings, bible study, Sunday service, feet washings, fish fries, and river baptisms. This was the traditional "sacred" means of escape from the hostilities of the world, and God was there. "If I ascend up into heaven," the psalmist says to God, "thou art there."

But blues people chose instead to make their beds "in hell." Actually, that "hell" was imposed upon them by the hostile world of the South. They simply chose not to escape from that world by submerging their sorrows in religion that was otherworldly, religion that taught church-goers to look for a better life in the world to come—in heaven. They chose instead to come face-to-face with the reality of their harsh everyday existence: They chose to make their beds "in hell." So, what "in hell" were they to do but sing the blues—that music of the human inner depths that told the truth about life as blues singers saw it, that music which revealed the full spectrum of their humanness? What "in hell" were they to do but to sing about how the rentman evicted them, how the bossman cheated them, how the lawman wrongly convicted them, and how their woman or man left them?

The Hebrews themselves had lamented that they could not sing the Lord's song in a strange land. Blues singers also lived in a strange land, a segregated and racist land, and they could not bring themselves to sing the Lord's song either. That is, they could not sing the Lord's song "in hell," but they could sing the blues. What "in hell" else were they to sing?

Like many of the Old Testament psalms and lamentations, the blues are songs that reveal the nitty-gritty details of life as it is lived at the underside of society and in the underbelly of history. Church songs do not reveal life's nitty-gritty or people's religious reactions to it, because they are comprised of predetermined doctrinal precepts. But the blues face up to life's nitty-gritty, and for some people pain and hurt cannot be assuaged by turning away from that ugliness and uncomfortableness with heavenly songs. For some people the only way to contend with life's difficulties is to look them in the eye, name them, bemoan them, curse them, and dance over them—in other words, sing the blues and amidst that seeming profaneness call on the name of the Lord: "oh Lord," "good Lord," "Lordy Lordy," "Lord have mercy," "the good Lord above," "my God," "God knows," "for God's sake," "I declare to God," "so help me God," "great God almighty!"

These familiar interjections found throughout the old country and city blues of the early part of the century seem to indicate that blues singers viewed God as present even amidst their blues lives. Indeed, the question of whether or not blues singers were ungodly seems really to hinge on whether or not God was there "in hell"—there in the juke joints and honky-tonks or wherever else the blues was played. The Psalm reads, "if I make my bed in hell, behold, thou art there." It does not say, "if I make my bed in hell, behold, the devil is there."

Perhaps singing the blues would not have been so requisite if the church had at least occasionally made its bed in hell. But since the church traditionally has not been there, blues singers should not have been expected to sing the Lord's song in a strange land. They should not have been expected to sing songs of rejoicing until they were in "heaven," until there was something concrete for them to rejoice about. When we "ascend into heaven" we can sing songs of thanksgiving and praise, for God is there. But when our beds are made "in hell" we ought to be permitted to sing the blues, for God is there too. To be able to sing church songs and the blues is to be truer to our humanness.

This holism I am referring to is also what makes for true monotheism. It is polytheism to say that God is present when people ascend into heaven and that the devil is present when people make their beds "in hell." Christians profess to be monotheists, so when we "ascend into heaven" and "thou art there" then what *in heaven* we are to do *is* sing the gospel good news; and when we make our beds "in hell" and "thou art there" then what *in hell* we are to do *is* lament and sing the blues. To be able to sing church songs *and* the blues is to be true to the wholeness of God.

But even though God will stay with us "in hell," to the very end if need be, perhaps it is ideal for us to return home eventually, as did the prodigal son in Luke 15:11–32. In Luke we read that the younger of two sons of a wealthy landowner took his inheritance and went into the world—"a foreign land"—and squandered it on riotous living. Eventually he had to sell himself into slavery and was sent by his owner to do the very lowly job of feeding swine. With little decent food to eat, the boy came to the realization that even the slaves of his father's household lived and ate better than he did. So he decided to return home and become one of his own father's slaves. Back home the son confessed that he had erred and that he no longer felt worthy to be called his father's son, but his father clothed him royally and prepared a feast in honor of his return.

So it is with blues people who return to the church. They have been on a religious sojourn to a "foreign land." They have lived "in hell" and returned "home" with the wisdom and the persona of people who have faced and pondered the hard realities of life. Indeed, the prophetic tradition that we see in the Old and New Testaments, the prophetic tradition epitomized in Jesus himself, can be attributed to the sojourner syndrome: the syndrome of those who were willing to leave the established institutions, including institutional religion, in order to go into the wilderness—a "foreign land"—and make their beds "in hell." But the significance of returning to the church is that it is evidence of a religious sojourn completed, of a reconnectedness to a beginning whence one has come.

This prophetic tradition did not embrace the eldest son, who had remained in the refuge of his father's home and had remained faithful to his father's household rules. This is evidenced by the fact that the elder son became angry that his younger brother was being welcomed back so festively. The elder son told his father that in the many years he had lived in the household, he had served his father well and had never transgressed. But the father, seeing his eldest son's anger, insisted that the family rejoice because the younger son had come back from "hell." The younger son, we see, had discovered his prodigality, but the older brother had not discovered his own. Blues singer Peetie Wheatstraw spoke to this paradox in his blues titled "The First Shall Be Last and the Last Shall Be First." The reason the last will be first is because to go and return is not only a special event worth celebrating, it is a sacred event. The circularity of the sojourn is as sacred as the ring of the ring-shout, whose circle represents unendingness, wholeness, fulfillment.

How can I celebrate those prodigal sons and daughters who had to make their beds "in hell?" I can celebrate them because, in the words of blues singers Robert Johnson, Son House, Bessie Smith, and Big Bill Broonzy, I myself preach the blues. I preach about coming to grips with the religious meaning of living *down here*—"in hell." With this "calling" in mind, I close with a most righteous passage from "Back to the Woods Blues," as sung or "preached" by bluesman Charlie Spand: "Just as sure as the good Lord sits in the heaven above, now your life ain't all pleasure unless you be with that one you love."

INTRODUCTION

The question of how best to re-search black music so that worlds of knowledge are not neglected was one of the motivating factors behind my Greenwood sermon notated in the foregoing prologue. The importance of this question is evidenced by the fact that it was the question that dominated the 1993 annual National Conference on Black Music Research, which convened in New Orleans, September 30 to October 3, a few weeks after my trip to the Mississippi Delta. Sponsored by the Center for Black Music Research, located at Columbia College in Chicago, the conference featured a round table discussion of scholars representing a myriad of the humanistic disciplines, including theater, poetry, literature, linguistics, art, dance, and music. The discussion was about what Samuel Floyd, Jr., founder and director of the research center, has termed "integrative inquiry." The approach to black music re-search that Floyd is trying to spawn under this category (with the help of the round table discussants) is re-search that hopes to propel black music scholarship beyond the standard approaches of historical musicology and ethnomusicology. This would occur through the embracing of a more culture-derived approach to re-search which would recognize the interdependence of the myriad humanistic disciplines in the study of black culture.[1] In Floyd's estimation, such an "integrative inquiry" might include the following culture-derived elements:

1) a system of referencing drawn from Afro-American folk music; 2) a tendency to make performances occasions in which the audience participates, in reaction to what performers do, which leads in turn to 3) a framework of continuous self-criticism that accompanies performance in its indigenous cultural context; 4) an emphasis on competitive values that keep performers on their mettle; and 5) the complete intertwining of black music and dance. These elements combine to create, foster, and define an artistic "field" that contains the foundational elements of calls, cries, and hollers; call-and-response devices; additive rhythms and polyrhythms; heterophony, pendular thirds, blue notes, bent notes, and elisions; hums, moans, grunts, vocables, and other rhythmic-oral declamations, interjections, and punctuations; off-beat melodic phrasings and parallel intervals and chords; constant repetition of rhythmic and melodic figures and phrases (from which riffs and vamps would be derived); timbral distortions of various kinds; musical individuality within collectivity; game rivalry; hand clapping, foot patting, and approximations thereof; and the metronomic pulse that underlies all African-American music.[2]

With regard to these "musical tropes" subsumed under the "master musical trope of call-response,"[3] Floyd put a specific question before the round table discussants: "Can they, or something like them, be applied also to inquiry into the other black cultural disciplines?" Stated differently, Floyd asked: "To what extent is it possible to formulate a common mode of inquiry, a single scholarship, for all African-American cultural studies—one that makes possible true interdisciplinary inquiry while also ensuring proper and appropriate recognition of the traditional boundaries and particularities of the various disciplines?"[4] In response to these queries, the thirteen discussants were each to make a two-minute introductory statement as an exordium to the round table conversation.

My opening remark was intended to contest Floyd's belief that "there has been no attempt to develop a comprehensive mode of inquiry that will make possible serious and significant artistic dialogue among scholars from all of the black cultural disciplines."[5] I found it necessary to contest the comment because I had written in the preface of *Theological Music: Introduction to Theomusicology*, my book of 1991, that part of what I intended to illustrate is that "theomusicology can, and at its best does, involve dialogue with different disciplines—folklore, literary criticism, sociolinguistics, biblical exegesis, and so forth."[6] Divinity scholar Clyde Steckel read the book and clearly understood my intentions. He writes, "Throughout the illustrative chapters of this book, where Spencer employs literary and musical examples of theomusicology at work, he makes clear that his goal, finally, is a process of intertextuality, placing the many and varied cultural constructs of all the disciplines of study into a mutual dialogue."[7]

In seven of the ten chapters in *Theological Music* I demonstrate this mutual dialogue. For example, in my chapter titled "Literature and Opera" I addressed linkages between the study of black music and the study of black literature, and named the same kinds of linkages Floyd later gave as an illustration of the veracity of "integrative inquiry."[8] I wrote:

> Black music has long helped literary critics understand black literature. [Donald] Petesch, for instance, turns to the spirituals to understand the forces in the black community that undergirded black resistance to racial counterforces. Just as [Paul Laurence] Dunbar drew on the spirit and rhythms of the slave songs—the spirituals and the seculars—so did the literati of the Harlem Renaissance draw directly on jazz and the blues. Because of this kind of symbiotic relationship between black music and black literature, it is important (at least instructive) for theomusicologists to borrow from black literature and literary criticism in their efforts to reconstruct the theological history of black people in America.[9]

Similarly, in my chapter titled "Criticism, Lore, and Linguistics," I stated that the integration of theomusicology with aspects of literary criticism, folklore, and sociolinguistics illustrates linkages between music and story—linkages of language, structure, formulaic idiom, and the scholarly criticism of these. I found it probable that sociolinguist Edgar Schneider and I could engage in a "common mode of inquiry," for Schneider had turned to the same sources of data that I had many times in my research. He examined some two thousand ex-slave narratives collected by the Federal Writer's Project in the mid-1930s and several sound recordings of blues made around the same time for the Archive of Folk Song at the Library of Congress. His intention to analyze the morphemes and linguistic constructions that make black English distinct from white dialects was certainly specialized, but his treatment of the unstressed verbal prefix *a-* was emblematic of possible mutual interests. The prefix *a-* is most frequently used with a progressive verb in predicate function[10]—"He was *a*-singin' a glorious song" or "They was jus' *a*-shoutin' to the music." With theomusicology as the mode of inquiry, Schneider might have found it possible to attribute meaning or function to the *a-* prefix. Crawford Feagin has suggested that the particle was meant to express intensified action, immediacy, or dramatic vividness,[11] but even here theomusicology might have permitted the linguist to see that the preverbal *a-* functions as a musical or rhythmic inflection intended to capture the surplus spiritual connotation of the verb's standard meaning.

From the musicological perspective alone, this interpretation is supported by the fact that in the singing of spirituals in dialect the *a-* coincides musically with the upbeat, giving the downbeat to the verb and stress to that verb's meaning. Adding the theological perspective, which William C. Turner, Jr., helps us do, the *a-* prefix seems to comprise the attempt of black speakers to capture the spiritual surplus of words that the English language uninflected is unable to convey. Speaking with regard to black preaching, where we would also expect to see this prefix, Turner says: "In the languages of West Africa precise meanings could be communicated through the rhythm and pitch of drumming, whereas the surplus of depth stirring within the African of the diaspora found limited correlation in the languages of North America. Black preaching, however, encompasses the atavistic and primal vocabularies of music. Being rooted in the primal nexus from which manifold expressions of African culture have traditionally effused, musicality in black preaching operates beneath the structures of logical communication and enhances the message spoken in behalf of God."[12]

What I am illustrating presently and illustrated previously in *Theological Music* incorporates but surpasses what Floyd only later concluded with regard to "integrative inquiry." Floyd says that perhaps music can be the "baseline discipline" in the quest for an "integrative inquiry."[13] Indeed it can, but not alone. The baseline discipline for an "integrative inquiry" must also include theology. Stating this publicly was part of the impetus behind my opening remark for the round table discussion on "integrative inquiry." So, first of all, I found it necessary to contest Floyd's belief that there had been no previous attempt to develop a comprehensive mode of inquiry that would make possible significant dialogue across black cultural disciplines. Then, secondly, I found it necessary to contest Floyd's belief that music alone can be that "baseline discipline." These two concerns led me to say this in my opening remark:

> In answer to Samuel Floyd's primary question, I believe it is indeed possible to formulate a common mode of inquiry, a single scholarship, for all African American cultural studies. I find my answer to be supported by two principles posited by Sterling Stuckey in his keynote address last night. First, with reference to Michael Harris's book, *The Rise of the Gospel Blues*, Stuckey mentioned the superficial nature of our division between the sacred and the so-called secular, given that African peoples have tended to view or treat all of life as sacred. Second,

Stuckey ... alluded to the centrality of rhythm in Afro-cultures: rhythm that is foundational in our music, dance, literature, and visual arts. If we accept these two principles as correct, then, first, the centrality of rhythm in Afro-cultural produce requires that we use musical language in order to discourse about it. This is evidenced in, for example, the literary criticism of Houston Baker and Henry Louis Gates and the art criticism of Robert Farris Thompson and Richard Powell. Second, the sacredness of all Afro-cultural produce requires that we use religious or theological language in order to discourse about it. The sum of these requirements—which is musicological inquiry that is theological—is what I have been terming *theomusicology* since 1987. I contend that musicological inquiry that is theological . . . is the kind of "single scholarship" being sought by "integrative studies."

Musicology and theology serving together as a singular baseline discipline for integrative re-search into black culture suggests, for instance, that literary critics who re-search Margaret Walker's *Jubilee,* Jamaica Kincaid's *Lucy,* Terry McMillan's *Waiting To Exhale,* Toni Morrison's *Song of Solomon,* Alice Walker's *The Color Purple,* or Charles Johnson's *Middle Passage* should also be able to speak to (and with the language of) the theologically informed musicologist who re-searches Bernice Johnson Reagon's *a cappella* group, Sweet Honey in the Rock, which performs spirituals, work songs, blues, gospel, jazz, civil rights songs, rap, reggae, calypso, and traditional African folk music. Scholars who re-search the African heritage of dance in the New World—from the ring-shout to the shout, from the cakewalk to the moonwalk, from the African dance of the Alvin Ailey and the Chuck Davis troupes to the dance of James Brown, Michael Jackson, and Hammer—should also be able to speak to (and with the language of) the theologically informed musicologist who re-searches the blues preaching of Robert Johnson and Bessie Smith, the jazz ballading of Ella Fitzgerald and Nancy Wilson, the folk singing of Richie Havens and

Tracy Chapman, the gospel musicking of the Winans and Take Six, the classical rendering of Marian Anderson and Kathleen Battle, and the classical composing of R. Nathaniel Dett and William Grant Still.

The art historian re-searching Jacob Lawrence's series *Harriet Tubman, Frederick Douglass,* and *The Migration of the Negro* must know with the theologically informed musicologist that Tubman and Douglass were singers of the spirituals: "O Canaan, sweet Canaan, I am bound for the land of Canaan." The migrating Negroes between 1915 and 1930 were often singers of the blues: "I'm tired of this Jim Crow, gonna leave this Jim Crow town; doggone my black soul, I'm sweet Chicago bound." If they were not blues singers or jazz musicians, they certainly were not simply common laborers or skilled or semi-skilled workers, but also gospel singers and whooping preachers. In either case, they were people of the ritual places of black rhythm—the church, the blues joint, and so forth. They were essentially people of dance, people whose heritage of African movement motifs found expression not only in the dance arena and the church but on the court and field and in the ring during the ritual play at sport. With Jack Johnson and Joe Louis heavyweight boxing became holy, but with Muhammad Ali the dance was manifest fully. Ali stands not only in the lineage of heavyweight champions Joe Louis, Ezzard Charles, Jersey Joe Walcott, Floyd Patterson, and Sonny Liston, but also in the tradition of pattin' juba, the Last Poets, James Brown, and Hammer; not to mention that his rhetoric stands in the tradition of Marcus Garvey, Malcolm X, H. Rap Brown, Elaine Brown, Angela Davis, and Public Enemy. Thus, the scholar of dance and linguistics, the political scientist as well as the sports critic, should all be able to speak "across disciplines" with that "common mode of inquiry" most fitting for black cultural re-search—theomusicology.

Certainly it should be left to scholars of black drama, poetry, literature, linguistics, art, dance, and so forth, to do theomusicology on their own particular subjects of interest and with their particular expertise. My intention in this book is not to attempt a cross-disciplinary dialogue with myself, but to extrapolate my exordium to the round table discussion on "integrative inquiry" at the 1993 National Conference on Black Music Research. Specifically, I will be contesting more fully Floyd's contention that there has been no previous attempt to develop a comprehensive mode of inquiry that would make possible significant dialogue across black cultural disciplines, and I will be contesting more completely Floyd's suggestion that music alone can be that "baseline discipline." In chapter 1, I will argue that African rhythm is foundational in black culture, in order to claim that the rhythmic nature of all Afro-cultural produce requires musicological language to discourse about it. In chapter 2, I will argue that religion is foundational in black culture, in order to claim that the sacredness of all Afro-cultural produce requires theological language to discourse about it. Once I have established these premises I have also established the basis of my claim that musicology and theology must serve together as the singular baseline discipline for "a common mode of inquiry" or "single scholarship" for all African American cultural studies.

I do not wish to stop there, however. I then proceed to demonstrate in my own area of re-search the results of engaging in this baseline discipline of theomusicology. So, I demonstrate theomusicology at work in my re-search of black folk, popular, and classical music in chapters 3, 4, and 5. All the while I explain in these three chapters the route by which theomusicology evolved, a trail that perhaps suggests a curriculum for the study of this "baseline discipline." In chapter 6 I will have returned full circle to my prologue, for I show that by engaging in theomusicological inquiry—whether on black folk, popular, or classical music—we cannot help but to discover an ethics that is as indigenous to black culture as "preaching the blues." This suggests to me that doing ethics should be integrated into every authentic act of "integrative inquiry." This last chapter thus answers the question in my foreword of how a scholar interested in re-searching black music arrives at the point where he can not only preach in church but preach the blues—not as a blues singer but as a musicologist.

CHAPTER 1

THE RHYTHM

In many traditional African societies the drum was a sacred instrument possessing supernatural power that enabled it to summon the gods into ritual communion with the people. In some societies drums were regarded as deities, deities whose voices were the percussive sounds that emanated. These drums, and all drums of lesser sacred status, performed a requisite function in the music accompanying ritualistic dance, for through the articulations of these instruments, drummers seduced dancers into ready fervor and mobilized the spirits into possessive action. The rhythm that did the seducing is characterizable in the singular as *African rhythm*, the singular intended to represent the common aspects of rhythm shared by most societies of continental Africa—first its sacrality, and secondly its multimetricity, cross-rhythms, asymmetrical patterning, and call and response, all articulated improvisatorially and percussively, especially upon the drum, and customarily concretized in dance.

Because the drums that articulated this African rhythm were important voices in African ritual and cosmology, it must have been a cultural shock when the drum had difficulty surviving some parts of the African diaspora. While there was continued use of the drum in the West Indies and South America, the instrument was essentially disallowed in North America by legal mandate due to the fears slave holders had of its ability to "talk." But while the drum was deferred in the diaspora, the drumbeats of Africa, I will argue in due course, endured the slave factories and the middle passage and were sold right along with the captive Africans on the auction blocks of the New World. Those drumbeats sat silent in many a gallery of white Protestant and Catholic churches, silent until they could "steal away" and release themselves without reproach in the physical concretizations of those who had carried the rhythm in the bones and blood and souls beneath their flesh.

African rhythm was the essential African remnant—the acme of Africanism, as I will show. Certainly the drum was a sacred instrument theologically pertinent to African ritual, but it was not so crucial an instrument that its absence prevented the continuation of such Africa-wide rituals as the ring-shout. In the New World this African dance, the first evidence of the drumbeats of Africa surviving the diaspora, was comprised of shuffling in a counter-clockwise circle to the beat of song with the feet hardly taken from the floor. One white observer of a shout on St. Helena Island, South Carolina, noted in 1862 that three men stood apart and sang and clapped while those who followed one another in the ring picked up tempo and momentum: "They began slowly, a few going around a[nd] more gradually joining in, the song getting faster and faster till at last only the most marked part of the refrain is sung and the shuffling, stamping, and clapping gets furious." The observer concluded by saying that the floor, which swayed regularly to the time of the music, shook so much that it seemed dangerous.[1] Around the same time and on the same South Carolina island, another white observer noticed that during the circular shuffling, which was usually but not always accompanied by singing, the dancers displayed a jerking motion that agitated their entire bodies.[2] Still another noted that there was a joining of hands by the ring-dancers.[3]

In each description of the shout's choreography, accompanying the dance is percussive rhythm articulated corporeally and consequential instances of spirit possession, which the dancers sometimes referred to as "getting the power" and being "filled with the spirit." As the Dutch historian of religion Gerardus van der Leeuw says of this generated power, "The dance, by its very nature, is ecstatic. It makes man beside himself, lifts him above life and the world, and lets his whole earthly existence perish in the maelstrom."[4] He continues, "This is what makes the dance as an art so broad and inclusive: the boundaries of the body and the soul open, and whoever dances feels how boundary after boundary fall away."[5] The ring-shout illustrates that in the absence of the drum other sources of rhythm were capable of summoning the spirits and mobilizing them into possessive action on the people so that the boundaries of the body and the soul are still able to open up.

In addition to the ring-shout, which during slavery generally occurred unknowing to whites, creolized African dance styles, maintained in the secret and public secular dance arenas of the enslaved, were also harbingers of African rhythms. In these secular dance arenas the movement motifs that were African were maintained and probably reinforced when newly imported Africans exerted a cultural influence on the plantations.[6] After slavery the African dance motifs in the secular dances found their way into the dances done in the jook joints in small towns of the rural South.[7] Since the jook was the only dance arena that accommodated the emerging culture of southern black freedpersons, it served as the common ground for the mixing of any remaining strains of African cultures along with those creole Africanisms that developed during slavery.[8] The dance styles of the jooks, which served rural populations of blacks, were proliferated by traveling black performers in the southern tent and medicine shows.[9] During the great migration, southern blacks brought these dance styles north. As the jook and its first urban progeny in the North, the honky-tonk, evolved into the urban after-hours joint, rent party, and black-owned club, the dances began losing their rural characteristics and the remnant of group dancing diminished in favor of individualized and increasingly sexualized partner dancing.[10]

But the African movement motifs, which were the corporeal concretizations of the creole African rhythms, continued, which is what I meant earlier when I said the drumbeats of Africa survived the diaspora. The dances nurtured on the plantations and later in the jooks and beyond (in the jook continuum) were but comprised of recycled movement motifs that could be traced back to Africa. For example, the dance called the itch, which can be traced back to the Winti people in Suriname (whose dancers tug at their clothing as though scratching), was incorporated into the breakaway of the lindy hop by the late 1940s, only to return as an embellishment to rhythm-and-blues dances of the 1950s.[11] The plantation dance called wringin' and twistin' became the basis of the twist, and the leg gestures of the Charleston appeared in the mashed potatoes of the late 1950s and early 1960s.[12] The hip gestures of the black bottom appeared as an embellishment in the lindy hop and jitterbug, and later in the mooche, and even later in the four corners of the late 1960s and early 1970s.[13] The camel walk, which can be traced back to Ghana, is a step similar to an Ashanti funeral dance called the Adowa.[14] Even the contemporary soul train line had its beginnings among many West African ethnic groups.[15]

So, while the religious places of worship were certainly important locations where the creolization of African rhythm occurred during and beyond antebellum times, the jook continuum was perhaps the portentous place of rhythmic creolization that has forever left its impression on the culture of modern times. As philosopher Alain Locke put it, slavery may have robbed Africans of their ancestral gift of fine craftsmanship but these artistic urges continued to flow into the channels of movement, song, and speech, and the body itself became black people's primary artistic instrument.[16] Locke's contemporary of the early part of the twentieth century, composer R. Nathaniel Dett, the well-known black arranger of spirituals, identified call-and-response and the pentatonic scale as prominent elements that reveal the African roots of black music. But Dett also said it was obvious that rhythm is what establishes the crucial link between the music of blacks and their African forebears, rhythm that is "reincarnated and re-christened" with each generation as syncopation, ragtime, jazz, and swing.[17] Composer William Grant Still, friend of both Dett and Locke, said he heard African rhythms not only in the spirituals and the blues but also in the Cuban rumba, the Brazilian samba, the Colombian bambuco, and the Haitian merengue.[18]

Obviously, the drumbeats of Africa endured the slave factories and the middle passage and were sold right along with the captive Africans on the auction blocks of the New World. Those drumbeats in turn survived urbanization, which depleted blacks of the environment of expansive nature, which in the rural South, as in Africa, was the chief conduit with the spirit world.[19] The drumbeats of Africa also survived industrialization, with its staid rhythms that, though percussive, beat counter to the asymmetry, multimetricism, and improvisation of African time. Having thus survived in the black folk and popular genres of music and dance, these drumbeats of Africa found their way into the sophisticated classical compositions and vocal performances of such musicians as Dett, Still, Roland Hayes, Marian Anderson, and Dorothy Maynor. This survival of African rhythms into modern times is the reason Locke was able to say of these black artists, that though they are thoroughly modern and their thoughts "wear the uniform of the age" their hearts yet "beat a little differently."[20] It is also of these artists that Locke is writing when he comments further about the kernel of African rhythm sprouting anew in the artistic soils of myriad diasporan lands, the point I promised to argue when I began this chapter:

> This racial mastery of rhythm is one characteristic that seems never to have been lost, whatever else was, and it has made and kept the Negro a musician by nature and a music-maker by instinct. When customs were lost and native cultures cut off in the rude transplantings of slavery . . . , underneath all, rhythm memories and rhythmic skill persisted to fuse with and transform whatever new mode of expression the Negro took on. For just as music can be carried without words, so rhythm can be carried without the rest of the music system; so intimately and instinctively is it carried. From this mustard-seed the whole structure of music can sprout anew. From a kernel of rhythm, African music has sprouted in strange lands, spread out a rootage of folk-dance and folk song, and then gone through the whole cycle of complete musical expression as far as soil and cultural conditions have permitted.[21]

So, despite the fact that urbanization depleted the urban North of the environment of expansive nature (that crucial conduit of the spirit world),[22] the hearts of the Negro Renaissance artists of the first and second post-slavery generations beat a little differently. In the case of the aforementioned composers and performers, it was the spirituals (for Still it was also the blues) that had left an impression upon them. Dett and Still recalled that they had heard their grandmothers sing the spirituals when they were children. When Dett, as a student at Oberlin Conservatory of Music, then heard the slow movement of Antonin Dvorák's "American Quartet," containing melodies from the spirituals, his heart beat a little differently. As he said in one of his essays under the fitting subheading "The Singing Dead," it seemed that he had suddenly heard the sweet voice of his long-departed grandmother calling across the years. In a rush of emotion that stirred his spirit to its very heart, he recalled, the meaning of the songs that had given her soul such peace was revealed to him.[23] Still must have had a similar heartfelt experience, for he remembered that his maternal grandmother, who lived in his mother's home in Little Rock, Arkansas, used to sing spirituals all day long. He also heard the spirituals and saw individuals doing the religious dance called the shout when he and his mother once visited a rural church. At that time the histrionic display humored him, but he later drew artistically from the experience of having heard black music at its authentic source.[24]

What Still probably heard at that church and remembered later on was not simply the African rhythms of the singing and the shouting but also of the preaching. The African rhythms of black preaching comprise the single ingredient that gives the melodiousness of traditional black sermonry both its momentum and its momentousness. Even contemporary black preachers, who have drawn artistically from the experience of having heard black music at its authentic source, continue to pursue the skill of improvisatorially fitting their phrases and sentences into quasi-metrical units. Accomplished by squeezing together and stretching out words in the same way that is done by the rap artist (who is the black preacher's contemporary linguistic kin), preachers often accompany this quasi-metered articulation by striking the lectern or stomping the foot. Thus, the "drumming" of traditional black preaching (like that of black rapping) includes kinetic, linguistic, and metric manifestations, which together create a polyphonic multimetricity equivalent to that of African rhythm. The consequence is frequently the eruption of extemporaneous song.[25] Gerardus van der Leeuw, being of a European culture, finds this fascinating, saying, "We can only long for a sermon which will so move us that the listeners can no longer control themselves but must shout, cry, and sing."[26] But in black culture, especially in the black church, such music, dance, and poetry are a unity and are common forms of expression for black people's feelings and thoughts.

It was probably their having experienced some aspect of traditional black singing, shouting, and preaching which led the Negro Renaissance artists to arrange and sing the spirituals and to return to the South to collect these folk songs at their authentic source. Dorothy Maynor recalled that though her teacher and mentor Dett was born in Canada and raised in the North, he had a yearning to learn about life in the South.[27] Maynor herself, and other artists such as Roland Hayes, also spent time in that ritual region gathering black folk songs from the nature that grew them. Hayes in fact went even further and spent substantial time studying African music. Having acquired a degree of technical knowledge about the music, he also had hopes of one day going to Africa for further study.[28] So, even though the Negro Renaissance composers and performers chose to work within the classical musical genres and had mastered the requisite skills to do so, their treatment of the spirituals was by no means de-spiritualized as many white critics believed. The same held true for Still's treatment of the blues within classical forms.

Though African rhythms wore the uniform of the age in the music of the Negro Renaissance artists, the drumbeats of Africa, though creolized, still beat a little differently. Indeed, the continuum of African rhythm in the New World remained so strong that this might have been the answer to the question W. E. B. Du Bois raised about what it was between his African ancestral homeland and himself that constituted a connection that he could better feel than explain: "Since the concept of race has so changed and presented so much of contradiction that as I face Africa I ask myself: what is it between us that constitutes a tie which I can feel better than I can explain?"[29]

To summarize, so that we may return full circle to the ring-shout for another tier of analysis, the diaspora generally de-drummed the enslaved Africans of North America but it did not de-rhythmize them. With the drum deferred in the diaspora, the percussive rhythms of "home" could still be manifested corporeally in handclapping, footstomping, and bodypatting. When corporealized in that most crucial African retention—dancing—the creole African rhythms produced, among other African-influenced choreographies, the ring-shout.

The ring-shout, as I now wish to point out, holds an especially important place in the New World continuum of African rhythm, because there was evidently a close connection between the ring-shout and the African trickster-god. Historian Sterling Stuckey says, "since tricksters, most notably the hare, pervade much of black Africa, as does the ring ceremony honoring the ancestors, and since the trickster and the circle are associated not only in South America where Africans were enslaved but in North American slavery as well, the evidence implies a wide association of the two in black Africa and, consequently, among numerous African ethnic groups in America."[30] The reason the association of the trickster with the ring-shout is so important to my project, as I attempt to comprehend the momentousness of black music, is that I interpret the trickster as the deity most representative of both the ritual place of rhythm-induced extradependence (church, blues joint, and so forth) and the personality of that extradependence. Like the tricksters of Africa and the New World who are embodiments of synchronous duplicity—both sacred and profane—the ritual place and personality of rhythm-induced extradependence is characterized by permissibility. This ritual place comprises experiences of gathering, greeting, singing, testifying, dance, trance, and collapse that are simultaneously spiritual and sexual.

It is in such rhythmic spaces at the ritual "crossroads" of the trickster—in both sacred and secular spaces—that a deep therapy of spiritual reintensification transpires. It is here that I wish to say that I disagree with Gerardus van der Leeuw's claim that the couple dance displaces ritual with lovemaking, resulting in dance becoming completely profane.[31] Specifically as regards black people, whose worship in the black church I described moments ago, I disagree with van der Leeuw's claim that the unity between dance and the rest of life is irrevocably severed. He states, "Today neither poetry, nor music, nor dance is a common form of expression for man's feelings and thoughts; rather, dance, like the other arts, is the talent of a small group and the pleasure of a somewhat larger one. Even purely as a form of entertainment, it gives expression—again like music—only to specific feelings, and those not exactly the most noble. In connection with religion . . . , it is scarcely alive, or not at all."[32] To contest van der Leeuw, in an attempt to contend that for black people the unity between religion and all forms of dance still exists (in reality though not in theory), I will draw on anthropologist Victor Turner. The power that black music is able to generate in the betwixt-and-between spaces of repressively "structured" societies seems to be by means of what Turner calls "antistructure" and its product, "communitas." Communitas breaks in through the cracks of structure in liminality, in at the edges of structure in marginality, from beneath structure in inferiority[33]—and, I might add, breaks in from above structure in spirituality. I surmise that the power that black people are able to generate corporately in those spaces within, beneath, beside, and above suppressive structures of society—those "crossroad" places that the trickster, because of his synchronous duplicity, is able to forge out for ritual—is the same power that black music-makers of the folk and popular genres are able to glean through embodiment of the trickster personality. This is exactly what black music-makers have done. Having first emulated the tricksters that they thematized in their tales, ballads, and blues, they eventually began to live those "tricky" lives.[34]

I am suggesting that it was not just the regular return to religious ritual (where the permissive spirit of the trickster dwells) that is so crucial to black people maintaining their religious cosmology and cultural peculiarities, but that there is a return to what I would like to call the trickster's rhythms. I am saying that while the sacred gathering places of black people are locations where people grasped by similar ultimate concerns unite to tell stories and sing songs about the content of those concerns, they principally return to these sacred gathering places to be grasped by the ultimate concern of rhythm. This return to and from African rhythms must therefore be understood as what philosopher Martin Buber calls the "two primary metacosmical movements of the world."[35] As social scientist Bruce Reed explains, the lives of religious people are characterized by an oscillation or swing between daily human intradependence and spiritual extradependence.[36] I suppose this means that an atheist (if there is such a person) is a person who does not "swing," given that I see the spiritual lives of black people as comprised of a normative oscillation from intradependence to ritual locations of rhythm. Otherwise, the theist and the so-called atheist are religiously the same, as Langdon Gilkey explains:

> This dimension in our world is not by any means simply or directly "God." Certainly it provides the region or the possibility of a relation to God, ... and for many and varied important reasons, Christians *name* this dimension or region of ultimacy by the symbol of God and define it further in terms of that symbol.... Here we are concerned only with the dimension as it is generally experienced, as it appears in and to our experience, not as Christians believe it to be and to be appropriately described. Ours is a phenomenology of the religious in secular experience, and it asks about neither the *reality* nor the ontological *nature* of that which lies behind or appears within the phenomena.[37]

So, whether sacred places or secular, rhythm provides both the pulse and the impulse hand-in-hand; and the experience of rhythm gives the people the reintensified strength needed to face again the structured and often oppressive workaday world.

I believe that the reintensifying rhythms in these ritual places leave a psychophysiological impression on each "worshipper," so that the impression appears in the black community as a kind of musical style which appears as charisma—that which distinguishes the persona and oratory of preachers like Martin Luther King, Jr., and Jesse Jackson. In other words, the rhythms of black music heard in black ritual places are heard and interpreted rationally, and they are felt physically via the vibrations of sound waves and the floor and furniture in those ritual places. I am arguing that the rhythms, which are heard and felt, are remembered long after they have died away in reality, and that they are acted out in ways that create what I call charisma. In addition, African diaspora scholar Leonard Barrett suggests that the impression of African rhythms also results in the self-confidence that fuels protest and insurrection:

> The restless rhythm of the African soul . . . was obvious to the white man from the day the Africans came ashore in the Caribbean until the day Emancipation was declared. It surfaced in the drums of the Maroons in the Cockpit Mountains of Jamaica; in the conch shells of the Haitians calling the barefooted soldiers to unite against the elite French regiments "steeled" by the drums of Vodun. It became a movement bound for the African homeland under Marcus Garvey's messianic leadership and later taken up by the Rastafarians. It escalated to a worldwide sound in the sixties in a holocaust of movements, the tremors of which still linger with us.[38]

So, the rhythms of black music heard in black ritual places are interpreted rationally and felt physically to the degree that the impression left on people results in the feeding of or even the fashioning of charisma and the kind of self-confidence that fuels social action. I will explain this further in a moment with reference to the work of psychologist Carl Seashore.

This means that had the slave traders succeeded in breaking the spirit of their captives in those slave factories on the West Coast of Africa—that is, had they contrived of some method of de-rhythmizing Africans—then there would have been no spirituals and no black church and no blues, no freedom songs and no freedom marches, no rhythm and blues and no soul and no black consciousness movement, no black theology and no rap. Had the slave owners, in an irrational act of desperation, enacted laws strictly forbidding their slaves not only to drum but to dance, sing, preach, pray, clap, stomp, sway, even to cradle their infants in their bosoms to the rhythms of their hearts that "beat a little differently"—and had they gone so far as to attribute those prohibitive laws to, say, the Apostle Paul—then after a generation or two they probably would have succeeded in breaking their captives. Confiscating the drum was certainly a cultural shock to the enslaved, but to have seized their rhythms would have been the ultimate act of dehumanization, indeed de-Africanization. Without their rhythms the descendants of the enslaved would have been a people without a cultural identity, the descendants of Ham would have indeed been cursed; and as rhythmless creatures, the notion that Africans had no soul probably would have convinced even them. But I have been arguing that the drumbeats of Africa endured the slave factories and the middle passage and were sold right along with the captive Africans on the auction blocks of the New World. Those drumbeats, creolized and corporealized, in turn survived urbanization and industrialization, thus solidifying a permanent place in black folk, popular, and classical culture. So, to repeat the very insightful words of Alain Locke, whatever African customs were lost in the rude transplantings of slavery, underneath it all "rhythm memories and rhythmic skill persisted to fuse with and transform whatever new mode of expression the Negro took on."[39]

Thus, the answer to the question anthropological archaeologist Leland Ferguson asks about black people's source of courage in the face of the historical deprivation of slavery and oppression is that blacks never forsook their reintensifying rhythms. Ferguson is already privy to the answer, for he says:

> However white Southerners and others responded to the Civil Rights Movement, one thing was true: it commanded respect. Black leaders were courageous, dignified, and articulate. But where did their strength come from? How was it created? Most whites could not say. . . . How could American Negroes—supposedly primitive at worst and poorly educated at best—gather the strength to fight the establishment and win? The answer, of course, was that beyond the eye and mind of the white majority, African American culture was vibrantly alive, and had been alive for more than three hundred years. Through that span, African Americans combined African legacy with American culture, and along the way they left stories in the ground.[40]

Martin Luther King, Jr., must have been one of the courageous, dignified, and articulate leaders of whom Ferguson was speaking. Having been at the forefront of freedom marches and mass meetings where music was a means of generating courage, King, revealing the theologian in him, wrote that both the rhythm and the words of the music were the sources of vibrancy among black people.[41] The words of song were perhaps important because they contextualized the rhythms by commenting on the specific events during the protests. But I contend that rhythm was the most crucial element. First of all, rhythm is required for the articulation and communication of the words of song. As van der Leeuw says, words exert a compelling force under rhythmic influence: "Where does the source lie? Surely not in the content of the words. At the magical, primitive stage, the beauty of words does not reside in their meaning, but in their rhythm, in their meter. The words generate a certain power which is fixed, controlled, and concentrated by the rhythm."[42] Van der

Leeuw would have said the same about rap music, for he states that words develop a concentrated power that is feared when they are metrically organized—strengthened by stricter control through repetition, rhyme, alliteration, parallelism, and refrain.[43] Van der Leeuw thus concludes that there is no basis for doing what theologians might wish to do in terms of giving words a preferred position in the relationship of human beings to the divine.[44]

In addition to the fact that rhythm is required for the articulation of words, so that those words can best convey their meaning, the real importance of rhythm is that it works at a more fundamental psychophysiological level. This is the aspect of rhythm that psychologist Carl Seashore says "gives us a feeling of power," the power to which I believe black people always oscillate in their search for extradependent reintensification. Of this rhythm Seashore says, "The pattern once grasped, there is an assurance of ability to cope with the future. This results in . . . a motor attitude, or a projection of the self in action; for rhythm is never rhythm unless one feels that he himself is acting it, or, what may seem contradictory, that he is even carried by his own action."[45] Van der Leeuw similarly states, "Rhythm literally sweeps everything along, and transfers itself to everything that comes under its influence."[46] Philosopher Kathleen Higgins identifies an ethical dimension to this sense of being "carried," a dimension resultant of one being swept outward away from self toward interaction with others. She says, "Music makes us feel ourselves to be connected with our larger social context. Because we respond to music physically, this connection is visceral as well as emotional. It is valuable to ethical living, for it extends one's sense of immediate concern beyond one's private person. It extends the range of one's identity by dissolving one's sense of a barrier between oneself and the rest of humanity."[47]

The points of van der Leeuw's, Seashore's, and

Higgins's analyses conjoin in the actual act of marching. We could again turn to the ring-shout, but let us instead use as an example the march, which during antebellum and postbellum years was a choreography that occurred at the religious meetings of blacks. According to Ella Clark, raised on her parents' plantation in Georgia, the ex-slaves who worshipped in the plantation church marched in pairs or in single procession to the beat of songs being sung; and the more rhythmically involved in the music they became, the more elaborate was their march. "I watched the leader as he rose in his dignity and poise," recalled Clark. "One by one his followers joined him. Perhaps Primus our blacksmith would lead a slow processional. Brer Squire the preacher would 'hist' the tune."[48] Howard Odum and Guy B. Johnson attempted to look past the external features of such choreography into the thoughts of the participants. In reading their thoughts, a reading probably based on songs they either had sung or could have sung, Odum and Johnson painted the spiritual landscape that probably gave meaning to the choreography. They said, "the Negroes often imagined themselves to be the children of Israel, while their marching songs represented Moses leading them out from under the bondage of Pharaoh, or they considered themselves as marching around the wall of some besieged city. Victory would be theirs sooner or later."[49] So, it would be correct to say, as King did, that together the rhythm and the words of the freedom songs were important.

However, I still contend that it was rhythm that was absolutely crucial to the movement, as to the Jamaican maroons in the Cockpit Mountains and to the Haitians whose conch shells called black soldiers to unite against the French. I believe musical texts were not always necessary to give rhythm a context, for, as Odum and Johnson illustrate, a mental image could be drawn from other sources. Walter Fauntroy, another courageous and articulate leader of the civil rights movement, demonstrated this when he borrowed biblical and hymnic imagery to portray the many civil rights marches in which he participated. He said that under King's leadership black people took their concerns to the streets and their instruments were their marching feet: "And they marched until the patter of their feet became the thunder of the marching men of Joshua, and the world rocked beneath their tread. ... And so, the decades of the sixties, I think, will go down as a classic example of the church of God 'marching as to war with the cross of Jesus marching on before.'"[50] But to proceed even further, even when a mental image is not drawn to give rhythm a context, rhythm, from van der Leeuw's perspective, creates its own context by impressing upon people a sense of the vaster world and the divine.[51] He says, "The innumerable demonstrations, meetings, witnesses, to which our social and political differences give rise, are actually only primitive forms of dance. ... The cause is not improved; not a single argument is advanced by a parade, not even when the parade carries banners and placards. But who will deny that power issues from these demonstrations. This power is directed both inwardly and outwardly. It strengthens the persuasive intensity and the spirit of the demonstrators, and concentrates an attack upon the offenders."[52]

Thus, the answer to the question whites had as to how blacks, uneducated if not primitive, could gather the strength to fight the establishment and win was that there was something beyond the sight and thoughts of whites that was vibrantly alive in black culture. That something, I am arguing, was the African heritage of rhythm. Through his archaeological study of the earthen story of seventeenth- and eighteenth-century southern plantations, Ferguson confirms that the material culture of enslaved Africans laid the domestic foundation for a culture that gave its black adherents "power." The material culture that was African-derived—tools, pottery, basketry, dwellings, and so forth—constituted the symbols of "power" that reinforced the views the enslaved had of themselves as Africans who were culturally distinct from their captors.[53] Ferguson says, "While many slaves may not have overtly resisted their enslavement on a day-to-day basis, most did ignore European American culture in favor of their own, and in doing so they also ignored and resisted the European American ideology that rationalized their enslavement. Archaeological research helps us see the contrast between the world the slaves built and the one they rejected."[54]

I contend that what the archaeological evidence reveals is that the social advances of the civil rights movement, as well as the black revolutions of the West Indies, came through a confidence derived from the African heritage of rhythm. The archaeological evidence also verifies that this rhythmic confidence was especially nurtured in the context of the religion whose ritualistic particularities it undergirds with a fundamental spiritual nature. For Ferguson says that engraved spoons and bowls excavated on low-country plantation sites, being evidence of African-style religious ritual, makes tangible his sense that Africans brought to the Americas not only a myriad of practical skills but also aspects of their traditional spiritual beliefs.[55]

Finally, the archaeological evidence reinforces my explanation of what I think Leonard Barrett means when he says, "The drum is Africa and the drumbeats of Africa were the prime method of Africanizing the New World."[56] What Barrett seems to be saying is similar to Paul Tillich's theology of culture, which holds that religion is all-pervasive in culture and therefore gives rise to culture. Tillich says, "Religion as ultimate concern is the meaning-giving substance of culture, and culture is the totality of forms in which the basic concern of religion expresses itself. In abbreviation: religion is the substance of culture, culture is the form of religion."[57] Bringing a musical hermeneutic to bear on this theology of culture (appropriate since I have already suggested that rhythm and the spirit are one and the same), I am arguing that African rhythms give rise to recurrent dominant traits in all black cultures. In fact, I am arguing that in the cultures of black peoples there are characteristics that black rhythms alone give rise to. These rhythms especially undergird and distinguish black musics, which comprise the fundamental source of movement, momentum, and momentousness in black religious ritual. This religious ritual is in turn the location in which black peoples absorb African rhythms and concretize them in other aesthetic ways that comprise black culture.

I have used the thoughts of psychologist Carl Seashore, anthropologist Victor Turner, archaeologist Leland Ferguson, philosopher Alain Locke, historian of religions Gerardus van der Leeuw, musicians R. Nathaniel Dett and William Grant Still, and dance scholar Katrina Hazzard-Gordon to explain what I mean by African rhythm surviving the middle passage and being carried culturally by black people in the modern world. With this argument now presented—that there is a fundamental rhythmicity underneath black culture, which at the very least requires us to use musicological language in order to discourse about that culture—I will now argue in the next chapter that black culture is thoroughly religious and therefore requiring of theological language to discourse about it.

CHAPTER 2

THE RELIGION

The work of Robert Farris Thompson, himself one of the discussants for the conference round table on "integrative inquiry," is an excellent example of the need for musicological language in black art criticism. In his book *Flash of the Spirit: African and Afro-American Art and Philosophy* (1983), in which he identifies Yoruba, Kongo, Dahomean, Mande, and Ejagham influences of West and Central Africa on the art and other visual traditions of African peoples throughout the New World, Thompson utilizes a musical hermeneutic which he explains in his introduction:

> Since the Atlantic slave trade, ancient African organizing principles of song and dance have crossed the seas from the Old World to the New. There they took on new momentum, intermingling with each other and with New World or European styles of singing and dance. Among those principles are the *dominance of a percussive performance style* (attack and vital aliveness in sound and motion); *a propensity for multiple meter* (competing meters sounding all at once); *overlapping call and response* in singing (solo/chorus, voice/instrument—"interlock systems" of performance); *inner pulse control* (a "metronome sense," keeping a beat indelibly in mind as a rhythmic common denominator in a welter of different meters); *suspended accentuation patterning* (offbeat phrasing of melodic and choreographic accents); and, at a slightly different but equally recurrent level of exposition, *songs and dances of social allusion* (music which, however danceable and "swinging," remorse-

lessly contrasts social imperfections against implied criteria for perfect living).

Flash of the Spirit is about *visual* and *philosophic* streams of creativity and imagination, running parallel to the massive musical and choreographic modalities that connect black persons of the western hemisphere . . . to Mother Africa.[1]

In the chapter titled "Round Houses and Rhythmized Textiles," Thompson's musical hermeneutic is most explicit. In terms of the Mande- and New World Mande–influenced cloths found in Georgia and Mississippi, he says of the "rhythmized, pattern-breaking textile modes" that the "spontaneity in design" (improvisation) constitutes a tendency towards "metric play and staggering of accented elements."[2] These designs, which he says are virtually intended to be scanned metrically, are visually resonant with the "off-beat phrasing of melodic accents in African and Afro-America music," a musico-visual idiom he says is unique to the black world.[3] Speaking summarily of the "visual sound" of the textiles found across the Mande-Atlantic world, Thompson states that, just as "multiple meter" distinguishes the traditional music of Africa, so does "emphatic multistrip composition" distinguish the cloth of West Africa and culturally related sites in Afro-America.[4] Elsewhere Thompson explains that he is not arguing that musical quality is consciously suggested by African textile-makers or that visual quality is solely African, but that it seemed to him that it would be irresponsible not to try to sharpen awareness of the patterns in African cloth by way of reference to corresponding off-beat phrasing of melodic accents in African music and dance.[5]

How did Thompson come by way of this musical hermeneutic and the insights it gives toward an answer to Samuel Floyd's question about the possibility of formulating a common mode of inquiry for African American cultural studies? In an interview Thompson explained that it was the rhythms of the African American hollers, blues, and jazz, and especially the rhythms of mambo that suggested his musical hermeneutic for African and African American art history: "If you look at my scholarship, it amounts, in many respects, to nothing more or less than glossing mambo through the history of art." Thompson continues, "Through mambo, African-Atlantic traits became my analytic system, a way of viewing the whole world. And it occurred to me: If *I* was moved, imagine how it hit Amiri Baraka. In fact, I think one could prove that mambo is a secret engine behind a lot of famous people."[6]

Thompson's explicit use of musical language helps capture the rhythmic essence that I believe underlies the cultural produce that is generally recognized as being aesthetically of African derivation. However, his development of an "analytic system" that glosses mambo should also have suggested the religious nature of all Afro-cultural produce, since the word *mambo* has religious meaning as well.[7] In terms of what Tillich says about the relationship between style and ultimate concern, I contend that African rhythm is a kind of meta-style that is connected with religion. Tillich says:

> The problem of style is one of finding what it is that these creations of the same style have in common. To what do they all point? . . . I would say that every style points to a self-interpretation of man, thus answering the question of the ultimate meaning of life. Whatever the subject matter which an artist chooses, however strong or weak his artistic form, he cannot help but betray by his style his own ultimate concern, as well as that of his group, and his period. . . . And in every style the ultimate concern of a human group or period is manifest. It is one of the most fascinating tasks to decipher the religious meaning of styles of the past such as the archaic, the classic, the naturalistic, and to discover that the same characteristics which one discovered in an artistic creation can also be found in literature, philosophy, and morals of a period.[8]

What Afro-cultural creations stylistically have in common, that to which they all point, is African rhythm. I contend that this meta-style, which transcends more particular styles like the archaic or cubic, points to a self-interpretation of black people that answers a question of the ultimate meaning of life: life is profoundly rhythmic like African music. Whatever their subject matter, no matter how strong or weak their artistic form, it is by this style that the ultimate concern of black art, and the group and period it represents, is manifest.

This argument about rhythm may appear ahistorical or unempirical in comparison to my use of psychology, anthropology, and archaeology in the previous chapter to contend that African rhythm survived the diaspora culturally. However, it is the nature of theology to be somewhat ahistorical (but logical) in presenting arguments. After all, the divine—for example, God—is not empirically provable by historical documentation, since no one has ever seen God or the divine—or rhythm, for that matter. So my interpretation of rhythm here is building on the comments of Gerardus van der Leeuw in the previous chapter, a theological interpretation.

I will explain this more in the coming pages, but only intend to make a simple point at present. That is, it was not necessary for Thompson to claim, as I have in the last chapter, that rhythm and religion are a unity, but simply to have recognized in his "analytic system" that the sacredness of all of life for black peoples also requires theological language. Since he did not do so, his implied theory for the inquiry into Afro-cultural produce approaches but never quite reaches the "true interdisciplinary inquiry" needed for African American cultural studies—theomusicology. As I argued in my opening remark for the conference round table and in the last chapter, the centrality of rhythm in Afro-cultural produce requires that we use musical language in order to discourse about it; but also the sacredness of all Afro-cultural produce, as I will argue in this chapter, requires that we use theological language in order to discourse about it.

Regarding the sacredness of all Afro-cultural produce, the first premise of theomusicology is that human beings are inescapably religious and therefore create art that is somehow expressive or representative of that religiosity. This may be a broad definition of religion to some scholars, but it will become clear as I proceed that my view of the inherent religiosity of human beings is set in the firmly established tradition of "theology of culture" theorized by Paul Tillich, his student Langdon Gilkey, and a host of other Tillichian students. The ethnomusicologist is one scholar with a more narrow or conservative definition of religion. I say this because the ethnomusicologist may allude to religiosity in music, but unless it is sacred music the ethnomusicologist hardly recognizes the presence of religiosity. For instance, Alan Merriam, who takes a strong anthropological approach to ethnomusicology, says, "In song texts, language is often more permissive than in ordinary discourse, and this can reveal not only psychological processes such as the release of tension, but information of a nature not otherwise steadily accessible. For similar reasons, song texts often reveal deep-seated values and goals stated only with the greatest reluctance in normal discourse. This may lead, in turn, to the discernment of an available index of the prevailing ethos of a culture, or to a sort of national character generalization."[9]

However, the first premise of theomusicology is Tillich's view that human beings are inescapably religious for the very reason that they are always concerned with "deep-seated values and goals." They always ponder the vital questions about life and death, good and evil, truth and falsity, origins and destiny, meaning and meaninglessness. Theologian Langdon Gilkey says these questions have been called "limit questions" because the answers to them are beyond verifiable knowledge, and have been called "ultimate questions" because they are unavoidable and the provisional answers we give to them are foundational for all that we are and do.[10] Gilkey's reference to "ultimate questions" is reference to Tillich's term "ultimate concern," about which Tillich says, "The unconditional character of this concern implies that it refers to every moment of our life, to every space and every realm."[11] Thus, Tillich says that to reject religion for the sake of the cognitive function of the human spirit is to reject religion in the name of religion because the search for knowledge is but the passionate longing for ultimate reality, and to reject religion for the sake of the aesthetic function of the human spirit is to reject religion in the name of religion because the aesthetic function is but the desire to express ultimate meaning. "You cannot reject religion with ultimate seriousness," concludes Tillich, "because ultimate seriousness, or the state of being ultimately concerned, is itself religion."[12]

Thus, the meaning of the prefix *theo* and the suffix *ology* in the word *theomusicology* is well put by divinity scholar Robert Shelton, who defines *theology* broadly enough to include his thinking about and dialogue with country music songwriter Willie Nelson. Shelton says, "theology—while the word literally means 'the study of God'—is at its heart about life, the meaning of life, the purpose of our existence. Theology is not merely some abstract theory about the nature and character of God. At best it is always related to life, life as we live it."[13]

The allusion that Tillich makes about human beings being inescapably religious generally would not be disputed as it regards black people. While modern human beings of western society want to declare themselves areligious, completely free of the sacred, such a claim generally would not be made by or about black people, who rarely try to disguise their faith out of an embarrassment for what others might consider a remnant of primitive society. The Ghanaian ethnomusicologist, J. H.

Kwabena Nketia, understands the implications of this as regards musicological analysis. In my discussions with him at the Department of Ethnomusicology and Systematic Musicology at the University of California, Los Angeles (UCLA), where he and I were visitors and shared lecture time in two different classes in November of 1991, Nketia admitted that though he has long opposed the fragmentation of musicology into "separate" disciplines, theomusicology seems especially appropriate for the study of African music. This is because, as he said in one of his lectures at UCLA, Africans have traditionally viewed all of life as spiritual. Nketia also said that because of the obvious cultural connections between African and African American music, the specialist in the latter should also be a specialist in the former. This suggests that he would also view theomusicology as an appropriate discipline not only for the study of African American music but for the study of all musics of the African diaspora.

There are scholars who would argue that any musicology that purports to hold the disciplinary secret to researching black music should be using indigenous tools only, and indeed they would have legitimate complaints. For instance, the field of anthropology is precariously steeped in all the problems attendant to privileged westerners studying, for the most part, non-Europeans from an attempted insider perspective. The consequence of what ethnomusicologist Bruno Nettl once identified as members of affluent societies studying the music of the poor is an almost inescapable conjuring up of Edward Burnett Taylor's "doctrine of development."[14] In his pioneer work in modern anthropology, *Primitive Culture* (1871), Taylor states that the art of "primitive cultures" reveals earlier stages of the high culture of Europe.[15] The practice of the privileged studying the music of poor societies still prevails today and remains tainted by Taylor's "doctrine," even though ethnomusicologists now resist being restricted to the study of so-called "ethnic," "non-western," or "traditional" music. Similarly, "mainstream" sociologists, using norms that are alien to the subjects of their study, have treated black peoples as aberrant groups that are disorganized and pathological. With their sociological theories and methods steeped in a "social problem" paradigm, a paradigm that is the progeny of Auguste Comte, sociologists apply such descriptions as "culturally deprived" and "socially disadvantaged." When social intervention policies and strategies result from such elitism and bias, the result is the kind of ill-conceived and condescending benevolence that scholars re-searching black music should avoid.

So, scholars who would argue that the re-search of black music should privilege indigenous tools make a legitimate point. But I also agree with Samuel Floyd that, in the search for analytical and interpretive strategies to help us understand black artistic expression, we must recognize that the exclusive use of black hermeneutic strategies without reference to the European side of the equation will result in incomplete analysis.[16] I do not think it is necessarily to the discredit of theomusicology, then, that from the time of its inception it has recommended the borrowing of thought and method from anthropology, sociology, psychology, and philosophy.[17] Each of these western disciplines has a musicological correlate with a heritage of ideation too rich to ignore. For instance, the ideation in the anthropology of music (ethnomusicology), the sociology of music, the psychology of music, and the philosophy of music is always suggestive of the religious, but the religious needs to be excavated and made explicit since social scientists and philosophers have sought to forget religion, to be completely rid of the sacred except as an artifact.

In borrowing from these disciplines the re-searcher of black music must be careful not only because these disciplines are steeped in the European world view, while black music is largely the product of a different or alternative world view, but for other reasons as well. The researcher of black music must also be careful not to allow the social sciences of anthropology, sociology, and psychology to overshadow theological diagnoses of culture with overbearing social scientific emphases and concerns. Similarly, the re-searcher of black music must be careful not to allow the discipline of philosophy, with its interest in universal questions, to overshadow the specific cultural perspectives of black people. For instance, Gerardus van der Leeuw explains that Arthur Schopenhauer's metaphysics of music, which does not permit music to be expressive of a specific joy or grief but always of a universal joy or a universal grief, causes the specificity of music to dissolve in universalism or foundationalism that poses as reality.[18] Van der Leeuw continues, "The reason that we ultimately discard the attractive theory of Schopenhauer is that we are not concerned with a metaphysics, but with a theology of music. Therefore, as was pointed out before, we may learn much from Schopenhauer, but we are not able to follow him. True reality lies for us, not in absence of images, but rather in the image itself."[19] I concur with Tillich that it is in "the image itself" that we find the expression of religion, insofar as there is no cultural creation that is without "ultimate concern" expressed in it.[20]

While it is true that the social sciences can be of service to the theological component of our re-search of black music by preventing it from losing touch with the mundane, theology can help the re-searcher overcome the unwillingness of the social science musicologies to learn from certain valuable traditions that are "nonscientific." Storytelling is one such tradition that has been of great import to black people worldwide, a tradition that we also find modeled in the blues and other secular forms of black expression and that is epitomized in the black church as testifying. Indeed, storytelling is as natural to black people as music-making itself, since religious faith is often requiring of self-reflexive or collective story.[21] However, from the perspective of the historical and social science musicologies, engaging in or doing theology on such narrative is intellectual apostasy.

These positive and negative views of narrativity, particularly of self-reflexivity, were represented at a forum I hosted on the topic of theomusicology at Bowling Green State University in September of 1991. The perspective of the social science musicologies was represented by Stephen Cornelius, who was one of the two ethnomusicologists invited to respond to the mixed panel of theomusicologists. Cornelius expressed deep discomfort with the self-reflexive aspect of each speaker's story: "I think that everyone who has gotten up here has spoken from their own personal perspective: 'This is why *I* am here; this is what interests *me*!' When we are too much in the personal we always run into the problem of how we relate the personal to the broader social. I am not saying that is not done or has not been done in the papers, I am saying that it is a question that ethnomusicology, for better or worse . . . , especially in its earlier days, tried to stay away from. They [ethnomusicologists] tried to look at things from the social in the broadest perspective." Cornelius concluded his admonition with a reprimand that illustrates how foreign storytelling is to those disciplines that are controlled by the social sciences. He warned the researchers at the forum to remain as "clear-headed" as possible and to try to keep the personal, social, and musical experiences separate from one another.

A response to Cornelius came from Nicholas Cooper-Lewter, a black psychologist and therapist whose musical "soul therapy" I will discuss in chapter 6 as an example of the ethical praxis that can result when we are willing to merge personal, social, and musical experiences. Cooper-Lewter said, "One thing you brought to my attention is that the . . . I/we orientation is quite different for you and for me. For when I think of 'I' it is really a 'we,' and it is relational. Therefore, as I hear you talk about

'Well everyone sort of came out of a personal kind of place and somehow we need to make sure we keep an objective distance,' as if the *personal* is of less value, that is a different kind of orientation.... [I] would say to you that if there is no *personal,* if there is no impact relationally, *then* it is of less value."

It was not long after our forum on theomusicology that I attended the 1991 meeting of the Society for Ethnomusicology in Chicago, where I discovered that it is when ethnomusicologists gather to discuss their discipline in a self-reflexive mode that they actually begin to engage in explicit religious talk like the re-searchers at the Bowling Green forum. This was evidenced in a session titled "Ethnics and Ethnomusicology," where a panel of six discussants had as their topic the work of non-white American ethnomusicologists and the impact of their ethnicity on fieldwork, ethnography, ethics, theory, and method. One of the discussants on the multiethnic panel, an Argentinean scholar named Carol Robertson, was especially direct about her discipline's devaluation of ideas regarding music's relationship to spirituality and about the avoidance of "sentimentality" in ethnomusicological scholarship. Robertson said that the academic discourse in which she had been working for two decades is sterile, hollow, and needful of the transformative capacity of self-reflexivity in ethnography, especially personal storytelling.

What Robertson was evidently referring to is the self-reflexive fieldwork account, which is being discussed among some anthropologists. In the self-reflexive fieldwork account ethnographers would not view the subjects of their inquiry as "other" or "ethnic" but rather would view themselves as "other." This heightened introspection would result in the ethnographers being induced to raise and ponder questions about themselves and their own cultures.[22] This need not be perceived as resulting in mere self-indulgence, for there are possible ethical consequences. This is an instance of something I cannot argue with empirical data, but only with logical argument. Philosopher Kathleen Higgins makes the point when she says, "the open-ended sociability of music puts us in touch with what is common to human beings across societies. The capacity to feel and to respond to musical stimuli is not limited to a particular group of people. By reminding us of our common human make-up, music serves a universal human function. Music locates us first within the human community, and only second in some cases within our particular society."[23]

A similar kind of ethnography, with equivalent possibilities for ethical reflection, is the postmodern ethnography, which results in "cooperative story." This is story that privileges a multivoiced dialogue rather than the monologue of the observer-observed text, and that results in the evocation of poetic or abstract mood and meaning.[24] This evocation of poetic or abstract meaning, produced by the juxtaposition of perspectives on the shared experience within a societal culture, is intended to free ethnography from the scientific rhetoric of "facts," "inductions," "verification," and the bogus notion that "ethnic" cultures can be capsulized when in fact cultures are always in transition.[25]

In recognizing at the conference session on "Ethnics and Ethnomusicology" that it was when ethnomusicologists were in their self-reflexive mode that they seem able to engage in explicit religious talk, I seemed to have discovered that personal or cooperative storying is actually requiring of theological conceptualization and language. I might even suggest that theology is the most direct archaeology to reaching the deepest channels of cooperative-reflexivity and self-reflexivity, since human beings, who are inescapably "ultimately concerned," must always return to or ultimately reach discourse about the vital questions.

The historical and social scientific musicologies could be expanded so as to include such narrative theology, but the theoreticians and practitioners of these musicologies have shown little willingness to modify their disciplines, perhaps because those disciplines would become not only something quite different from what they have been traditionally but because they would become perceptibly "unscientific" and "ahistorical." As ethnomusicologist Philip Bohlman admits, "Identifying the presence of the religious in music would seem, in fact, to challenge the usual categories and constructs with which we commonly interpret music."[26]

The perception of western musicologists that theology is unscientific is illustrated by historical musicologist David Burrows, who begins his musicology under the assumption that there are three "fields" of musicological interest. *Field 1* is the realm of physical space that is within reach of the senses.[27] It appears that this field implies that the anthropology and sociology of music are the most fitting forms of scholarly inquiry. *Field 2* is the realm of thought and reason that reaches beyond the limitations of physical space.[28] This implies that the psychology and philosophy of music are the most fitting forms of inquiry. *Field 3* is the realm of the spirit that reaches beyond the limitations of the intellect, a field approximated by human participation in religion and mysticism.[29] This seems to be the primary field of interest for theomusicology. Now, to make my point regarding the traditional tendency of musicologists to avoid or even to shun theology, Burrows says that "field 3," though related to religion and mysticism, is not intended to be understood in a primarily theological way.[30] Yet Burrows can only "imagine" a way of dealing with what he calls the "momentousness of music" (no doubt a "field 3" manifestation) because such a method would require too great a subjective approach (no doubt the approach of theology).[31]

Seemingly implicit in Burrows's thought is the basic idea behind Auguste Comte's "great law of three stages," which Comte believed characterized the developmental course of human intelligence. Comte says that each branch of human knowledge evolves through three theoretical phases: the theological or fictitious, the metaphysical or abstract, and the scientific or positive.[32] Through this lens it appears that Burrows similarly implies intellectually digressive movement in his sequence of fields and in the required scholarly approaches to each field: "field 1" the scientific or positive, "field 2" the metaphysical or abstract, "field 3" the theological or fictitious. This devaluation of the theological is prohibitive of thorough research, for I believe Langdon Gilkey is irrefutable in his claim that even the most objective attempts at history-writing are at best projected hypotheses, studied guesses, and matters of communal commitment and hope, so that history is actually requiring of mythological and theological understanding.[33]

Even if western musicologists were willing to back off of the scientific and demonstrate a willingness to grapple with the metaphysical aspect of music's momentousness by way of the philosophy of music, they still will not have gone quite far enough. As I will explain in chapters 4 and 5, they will not have gone far enough in trying to understand how religious human beings themselves conceptualize the momentousness of their music and music-making experiences. There is certainly some value to understanding, for instance, Arthur Schopenhauer's philosophy of music. While we might outright disagree with his claim that of all the arts, music alone is the immediate language of "the will," the will being that ontological entity that is the essence behind all reality in objectification,[34] we would certainly benefit in our attempt to understand the music of Arnold Schoenberg since he appropriated Schopenhauer's metaphysics as the basis of his ultramodern twelve-tone composition. Musicologist John Covach explains:

Schoenberg is known to have studied Schopenhauer's work carefully, and it is especially Schopenhauer's aesthetics of music that bear upon the present discussion. It is well known that Schopenhauer divided our knowledge of the world into two aspects—the world as representation and the world as will. Responding to Immanuel Kant's claim that we are restricted in our knowledge of any object by our manner of representing things to ourselves (that is, we can never know what things in the external world are really like, but only how they appear to us), Schopenhauer posited that we can in fact come to understand these "things-in-themselves." The Kantian thing-in-itself is something Schopenhauer calls "the will." The will exists outside of time, space, and causality (these being a priori modes of our internal representation). As such, the will is absolutely unified, though it is subject to various degrees of objectification. While the other arts capture these various degrees of objectification of the will through the Platonic Ideas, music captures the will directly, in a manner that has no need of the Ideas. Music thus provides the most accurate representation of the will.

Schopenhauer's aesthetics of music do not support the idea that a musical work creates a world of its own but rather suggest that music offers a kind of best-possible access to the real thing-in-itself, the will.[35]

But, still, to go this far in the study of even Schoenberg's music is not to go far enough, for the language of metaphysics is merely a smoke screen for the theological world view of human beings who try to forget religion consciously but who remain inescapably religious in the Tillichian sense.

Thinking back on the position of Nketia, there is especially no need in the re-search of black music to presume the dominance of "field 1" and "field 2" manifestations (the scientific and the metaphysical) when the momentousness of this music cries out to be read in a theological way. Perhaps black music cries out thus due to the fact that black music itself is, from an Afro-conceptual viewpoint, theological sound. Bruno Nettl says that in certain African societies the sound of music was often identified with the voices of deities,[36] yet no musicologist to my knowledge has given any consideration to the possibility that perhaps what music is from such an Afro-conceptual viewpoint is sound (rhythm) that is unconsciously perceived of as being religious. This would account for the conceptual momentousness of black music to black people and the potency it has to heal and empower.

So, re-searchers of black music, as Nketia agreed earlier, must engage in the study of the theological. I am contending further, now, that those who would comply cannot be satisfied with the perspective of theology being merely tolerated as though the vital questions and ultimate concerns and the mythologies and mystifications of religious human beings are unworthy of serious scholarship on their own grounds. The re-searcher of black music should not be hesitant to proceed under the assumption that the provisional answers that we find for our vital questions are foundational for all that we are and do, and that these mythologies and mystifications of the cultures being studied make up the indigenous and therefore normative sources of understanding those cultures. Besides, though the re-searcher of black music may privilege "field 3," there is still room in this spiritual archaeology for social scientific inquiry. It is just that this scientific component should be applied with the understanding that its insights are often outside what is normative in the world view of the community of religious human beings being studied.

While theomusicology permits the mythologies and mystifications of cultures being studied to comprise the indigenous and therefore normative sources of scholarly understanding and is therefore less reductive of that which it is studying, the other musicologies have not followed this precept and so have been very much reductive of the momentousness of black music. The kinds of questions these other disciplines permit to be raised and addressed with regard to black music are so limited as not to include the questions and concerns that the indigenous creators and consumers of black music have consciously or unconsciously asked themselves in their everyday existence as religious human beings, indeed as religious human beings whom Nketia agrees tend to view the world as thoroughly spiritual.

In summary, with the close of this chapter I have argued the two premises that I posited at the round table discussion on "integrative inquiry" at the 1993 National Conference on Black Music Research. In chapter 1 I have argued that the centrality of rhythm in Afro-cultural produce requires that we use musicological language to discourse about it, and in chapter 2 that the sacredness of all Afro-cultural produce requires theological language to discourse about it.

I have provided historical documentation where possible, but to do theomusicology is not always or even necessarily to do history. It is the nature of theology, which is at the base of theomusicology, to be ahistorical (but logical) in presenting arguments. After all, the divine (including God) cannot be documented empirically as existing. Only logical arguments can be given for the possible existence of the divine (and God). So, if I have adequately argued the two foregoing premises of chapters 1 and 2 then I have shown that the sum of the requirements of theological and musicological language is *theomusicology*, and that theomusicology is the single scholarship being sought by "integrative studies" for an ideal re-search of black music. Let us apply these premises to the re-search of black folk, popular, and classical music in the next three chapters to see if they hold true and to see what is revealed. Having argued for the indigenous nature and theological value of storytelling, I will take the liberty to be self-reflexive at fitting moments, including the opening of the next chapter.

CHAPTER 3

FOLK MUSE

I have been studying black music seriously since my undergraduate and graduate school years, but my earliest *research* of black music commenced when I decided that my interests necessitated supplementing my training in music with training in Christian theology. I thought that, if the creators of black sacred music were Christians who drew from their life experiences as interpreted through the biblical lens, then how else could I expect to derive a more informed re-reading of their music without such study? For instance, the spirituals and the black preaching event out of which many spirituals were spontaneously created clearly called for the integration of theology into the general field of musicology.

In my re-search on black preaching, which came first, I found that a perspicuous correlation existed between black preaching and the spiritual, in that it is most probable that a substantial number of spirituals evolved via the preaching event of black worship. Although it is likely that, apart from worship, slave preachers worked at composing pleasing combinations of tune and text to later teach their "spirituals" to their congregations, it is probable that the more frequent development of spirituals came from extemporaneous sermonizing which crescendoed little by little to intoned utterance. This melodious declamation, delineated into quasi-metrical phrases with formulaic cadence, was customarily enhanced by intervening tonal response from the congregation. Responsorial iteration of catchy words, phrases, and sentences resulted in the burgeoning of song, to which new verses could be contemporaneously adjoined. Spirituals created in such a manner were sometimes evanescent no doubt, while favorable creations were probably remembered and perpetuated through oral transmission.

This information was deducible from the historical-musicological work of combing the manuscript pages of plantation diaries, journals, and correspondences and the ex-slave narratives systematically collected during the 1930s. But to contend authentically with the musicality of black preaching would require me to traverse the realm of inquiry that reaches beyond the limitations of the intellect, a realm approximated by human participation in religion and mysticism—David Burrows's "field 3." As theologian William C. Turner, Jr., says in his foreword to my book on the musicality of black preaching, *Sacred Symphony: The Chanted Sermon of the Black Preacher* (1987), "the dominant forces in American culture, greatly influenced by the Enlightenment and the rise of modern science, offer little support for a form of preaching infused with the mystical potency of music. Perceived by teachers of preaching and authors of homiletical texts as an aberration of Christian orthodoxy, this peculiar style of delivery is considered to be a vestige of 'folk religion.'"[1]

While in *Sacred Symphony* I was able to do the historical-musicological work of documenting the musicality of black preaching from antebellum times, and the ethnomusicological work of collecting, transcribing, and theoretically analyzing contemporary instances of musical black preaching in order to show the continuity of this tradition, I was not yet able to engage in spiritual archaeology. So I asked Turner to write a foreword to *Sacred Symphony* that would get at the theological depths, which even in my neophyte theological thinking were implicit in the musicality of black preaching. Turner did so and identified three ways of understanding the musicality of black preaching as religious. His arguments are not empirical or historical ones that can be documented. They cannot be documented, for they are the mere attempts of the religious human being to make sense of the religious sensation that he and other black people feel during the preaching event. But in his attempt to argue theologically for a rationale for this sensation, he spoke of the musicality of black preaching as kratophany, as oppugnancy, and as glossa. On the musicality of black preaching as kratophany, he wrote:

> Within the Black Church tradition, preaching is truly a manifestation of power or a "kratophany." As in a theophany, which is a manifestation of deity, some object is present which opens to the transcendent while simultaneously being rooted in empirical reality. With a theophany, the object may be a tree or a stone, as in African traditional religions, while with preaching, the kratophany is spoken word and rendered gesture. Further, within the context of the culture that sustains black preaching, there is no modality more indicative of the presence of deity, power, and intrusion from another order than that of the preached word circumscribed by musicality. In a stalwart way, music is one of the instruments bridging the chasm between the world of human beings and God who speaks to them through preaching. Music in black preaching establishes a direct link between the spirit within the preacher, the word that is uttered, and the worshiping congregation. It operates beneath the structures of logical discourse and produces a captivating effect upon the hearer.[2]

With regard to the musicality of black preaching as oppugnancy, Turner stated in his foreword to *Sacred Symphony*:

> The presence of music within the African world view corresponded to the oppugnancy African-American slaves had toward the world. To Africans, music was "numinous": it was the property of the deities and it manifested the most primal force in life. As a structuring principle for all reality and an inner force

that yielded life and unity, music moved the community backward, away from the reality of the present into the time of the deities. The same atavistic influence operated upon the adherents to Afro-Christian faith. The content and musicality of black preaching moved hearers away from the history that had unleashed terror upon them.

The direction of black preaching itself has ever been away from the world of oppression and poverty. . . . Only through perpetuating their quarrel with history while simultaneously sidestepping its terror could they forge a positive identity for themselves. Homiletical musicality and the songs which that musicality produced correspond with the content of the message of black preaching as a "gesture away from history"—an affirmation of the atavistic, the primal, and the world God has truly willed.[3]

Finally, with regard to the musicality of black preaching as glossa, Turner wrote:

In black religious folklore there is also the notion of "moaning so the devil won't know what you are talking about." Conversely, the Spirit prompts and discerns such inarticulate speech (glossa) and grants interpretation of the same.

Hence, the music of black preaching can be understood as a sort of "singing in the spirit," for there is a surplus (glossa) expressed in music which accompanies the rational content (logos) enunciated in words. The logical portion is contained in the structure of the sermon and the form of its constituent songs. For the glossal portion, the preacher becomes an instrument of musical afflatus: a flute through which divine air is blown, a harp upon which eternal strings vibrate. In attaining this height of musicality, "the preacher has come."[4]

In writing his foreword to my book, Turner demonstrated to me early on in my theological training the importance of integrating theology into musicology in the re-search of black sacred music. With a deeper understanding of the spirituals themselves as my next endeavor, I decided I should follow Turner's paradigm and apply to my analysis of the spirituals tools gleaned from formal theological training. My models were Henry Hugh Proctor's

Yale Divinity School thesis titled "The Theology of the Songs of the Southern Slave" (1894),[5] Howard Thurman's *Deep River* (1945) and *The Negro Spiritual Speaks of Life and Death* (1947), and James H. Cone's *The Spirituals and the Blues* (1972). Later I added to this list two unpublished essays of historian Earl E. Thorpe. While teaching history full-time and studying theology part-time during the early 1980s, Thorpe wrote two exemplary "integrative" essays—"African Americans and the Sacred: Spirituals, Slave Religion and Symbolism" and "Slave Religion, Spirituals, and C. G. Jung." The former was written for a course Thorpe took on "Myth and Symbols" with Duke Divinity professor H. B. Partin, a former student of the historian of religion Mircea Eliade. The latter essay is the product of Thorpe's integration of musicology, theology, and psychology in an effort to broach the minds of the enslaved Africans in America and the psychological matrix of the South that was responsible for the conditions that produced the spirituals. I will discuss this latter essay because it foreshadows my coverage in chapter 6 of Nicholas Cooper-Lewter's integration of musicology, theology, and psychology into an ethics and therapeutic praxis.

Thorpe begins his essay titled "Slave Religion, Spirituals, and C. G. Jung" by saying that his theoretical goal is to substantiate that Jung's psychoanalytical theories comprise a viable tool for deciphering the deepest feelings and unconscious beliefs of the Africans enslaved in America.[6] He says that just as Jung's principal purpose for psychotherapy was not to transport patients to an unattainable state of happiness but to help them acquire a mechanism for perseverance in the face of suffering, so did the enslaved seek to attain a similar state of mind. In fact, Thorpe goes so far as to suggest that the spirituals were evidence that the enslaved actually possessed the mental health and spiritual wealth that Jung's patients sought. By no means simply an opiate, insists Thorpe, the religion evidenced in the spirituals carried the enslaved to an essential stage of mental well-being. Pointing as an example to Jung's belief that prayer reinforces the healing potential of the unconscious, Thorpe says the creators of the spirituals also had faith in the power of prayer and that many of the spirituals were actually the enslaved praying aloud. While in psychotherapy patients tell the physician all about their anxieties, in the spirituals the enslaved told God all about their troubles. With regard to what I will discuss further in chapter 6, Thorpe's "integrative inquiry" caused him to stumble onto what Paul Tillich theorized about with regard to theology and psychotherapy being strikingly analogous in their methods of mental healing and traditional ideas about personal salvation: that both are "therapies" of grace which involve the overcoming of guilt and estrangement.[7]

My understanding of the therapeutic implications of Thorpe's re-search on the spirituals would come later in my theological education, as chapter 6 will tell. Initially I was simply impressed by James Cone's treatment of the spirituals from his purview as a systematic theologian who did "liberation theology." I found Cone's theology to be a distinct advancement over Henry Hugh Proctor's treatment of the spirituals as emblematic of "noble Christian sentiment," perfect in their biblically based doctrines about God, Christ, the holy Spirit, angels, Satan, the Christian life, and eschatology. I also found Cone's theology to be a distinct advancement beyond the imperceptibility of such white scholars as Robert Gordon. In a 1932 essay on the spirituals, Gordon showed an unwillingness or inability to recognize not only the originality of the spirituals but to recognize that they were inherently songs of liberation. He wrote:

> The entire concept of spiritual slavery, of the bonds and shackles of sin, of Pharaoh and Moses, and the Red Sea . . . is to be found expressed in minute detail in any number of hymns of demonstrable white origin, often in the identical words used by the negro in his spirituals. On the other hand, the total number

of cases in all the known spirituals of the negro in which we can be certain that he refers to physical and not to spiritual slavery can almost be counted on the fingers. Among them are, of course, "No More Auction Block for Me," "No Driver' Lash in de Heaben, O Lord," and a very few others.

I do not mean to imply that the negro did not often see in such white songs the possibility of a double meaning, that he did not in his own mind apply whatever he adopted from these songs to physical, as well as spiritual, slavery. But he did not himself create any body of song on his enslaved condition.

He found in white hymns, as commonly sung, fully developed ideas concerning spiritual slavery, the Last Judgment, and the joys of Heaven. These he used as a basis of song building. ... In no case did he change greatly the basic concept, present it from any new point of view, or introduce to it any new philosophy. He reexpressed the borrowed concept in his own way.[8]

Gordon evidently projected the heroic David and Samson types into the New Testament, so as to interpret the Old Testament liberation dramas with a Pauline hermeneutic, an otherworldly rather than thisworldly eschatology.

Because Cone was able to see through the mask of Christian nobility and piety and realize that the spirituals had picked up and protracted that prophetic strain of the biblical text which mandates that the oppressed be set free, I decided I should formally study liberation theology. In doing so, I discovered that the slave narratives fully corroborated Cone's liberationist reading of the spirituals and of the biblical source from which the theology of the spirituals came. For instance, Solomon Northup, in his autobiographical *Twelve Years a Slave*, said that if we could only know the secret thoughts of the enslaved, thoughts never uttered in the hearing of whites, we would find that ninety-nine out of every hundred of the enslaved were intelligent enough to understand their predicament and to cherish freedom as passionately as all other human beings.[9] Frederick Douglass, in his autobiographical *My Bondage and My Freedom*, stated similarly that every tone in the spirituals was a prayer to God for deliverance from slavery (verifying Turner's notion of musicality as oppugnancy), and that a keen observer might have detected in their songs about being "bound for the land of Canaan" that the enslaved were not first interested in going to heaven but in reaching the North.[10]

Cone's re-search helped me see that in their spirituals the enslaved were literal in their interpretation of the Old Testament liberation events. When they sang "Go Down, Moses," for instance, they were thinking about liberation in this world and thus singing with real anticipation:

> When Israel was in Egypt's land
>   Let my people go,
> Oppressed so hard they could not stand,
>   Let my people go.
>
> "Thus spoke the Lord," bold Moses said,
>   Let my people go,
> If not I'll smite your first born dead,
>   Let my people go.
>
> REFRAIN
> Go down, Moses,
> 'Way down in Egypt land,
> Tell ole Pharaoh,
> Let my people go.

Although being physically "let go" was the ideal attainment of liberation for the enslaved, Cone also argues that the freedom they sang about included but did not depend on historical possibilities.[11] He uses the spiritual "Oh Freedom" to make his point:

> Oh Freedom! Oh Freedom!
> Oh Freedom, I love thee!
> And before I'll be a slave,
> I'll be buried in my grave
> And go home to my Lord and be free.

This spiritual suggests to Cone that freedom for the enslaved included but did not depend on historical possibilities. He explains:

> Here freedom is obviously a structure of, and a movement in, historical existence. It is black slaves accepting the risk and burden of self-affirmation, of liberation in history. That is the meaning of the phrase, "And before I'll be a slave, I'll be buried in my grave." But without negating history, the last line of this spiritual places freedom beyond the historical context. "And go home to my Lord and be free." In this context, freedom is eschatological. It is anticipation of freedom, a vision of a new heaven and a new earth. Black slaves recognized that human freedom is transcendent—that is, a constituent of the future—which made it impossible to identify humanity exclusively with meager attainment in history.[12]

Looking through this very same hermeneutical lens provides us with one way of interpreting the many "train" songs that are found in the repertoire of the spirituals. On the one hand, the real-life liberating activity of the underground railroad seems to be thematized, but on the other hand there also seems to be an inclination toward not holding liberation to historical possibilities. One such "train" spiritual had the enslaved singing that the "same train" that carried away their mothers and sisters would "be back tomorrow." Everyone was encouraged to pack their bags in preparation, for though the train was due on the morrow it could pass through any night:

> Little black train is a-comin'
> Get all your business right;
> Go get your house in order,
> For the train may be here tonight.

My formal study of liberation theology was helpful in allowing me to see how it is possible to move from the Bible as canonical source of authority to liberation theology. But to follow Cone's knowledge also necessitated that I study formally the Old and New Testaments. This work pushed me beyond an uninformed literalist reading of the Bible as a volume comprised of a homogeneous history, doctrine, and theology. As a result, I was able to take interpretative control over the Bible, the kind of interpretative control that enabled Paul Tillich to fashion his theology of culture and begin reconciling aspects of our humanity that are not strange to one another but which have been estranged from one another,[13] the kind of interpretative control that eventually enabled me to preach the sermon that comprises my prologue.

Thus, what black biblical scholar Vincent Wimbush says of the importance of black Christians gaining interpretative control over the Bible became, in my estimation, equally true for the scholar interested in re-searching black sacred music. Wimbush says, "Needed are both a defense from alien, imperialistic hermeneutical constructs (and with them symbols, concepts, rituals, social orientation) and the capacity to assume control over, to evaluate critically, and advance their own traditions. . . . Critical facility for the historical study of both the self, viz., the Afro-Christian tradition, is required for self-defense and self-criticism, as well as the capacity for the construction of a more affirming, indigenous hermeneutic built on the tradition."[14] Wimbush concludes with a comment that reinforced my sense that formal study of the Old and New Testaments was important to my ability to understand and do liberation theology. He says that what liberation may initially require is "exegetical room."[15]

To be sure, re-search into black sacred music, music that has always been under the canonical authority of the biblical tradition, is also needful of "hermeneutical control" and "exegetical room." Without this "control" and "room" our conclusions about the meanings of the spirituals, meanings that Cone has proven to be masked, would be incorrect like Robert Gordon's interpretation of the spirituals, or only partly correct like Henry Hugh Proctor's interpretation. With this "control" and "room" and the almost certain discovery that there is no historical, doctrinal, or theological homogeneity in the Old or New Testament, comes the possibility that a spiritual archaeology of music can excavate more freely and much more deeply. As I will point out in my last chapter, in a final explanation of the implications of my prologue, it is the lack of "hermeneutical control" in our scholarship on black music that has suffocated all kinds of possibilities for the development of an ethics indigenous to black culture.

The first consequence of my learning the Bible and taking "hermeneutical control" over it is that I was better able to follow Cone's liberationist reading of the spirituals. The second consequence was that I was able to follow Cone's argument for the likeness between the spirituals and the blues. This comprised my earliest impetus to push my scholarship beyond the re-search of sacred folk music to include secular folk music. I was able to corroborate through my own re-search Cone's contention that the early blues were neither irreligious nor anti-religion. I was able to accomplish this in part with the help of Nicholas Cooper-Lewter's and Henry Mitchell's idea that there is a natural "soul theology" in the black community, a natural law that is inherent to the cultural expressions of the black community.[16] The substance of this soul theology comes from the hymns, spirituals, gospel songs, and anthems of the church, as well as from the blues outside the church.[17] This natural "singing system" is ultimately one in which the folk of the soul community maintain a wholesome existence free of external (professional) therapy due to their intuitive selection of songs that provide them with the internal nourishment and nurturance they need.[18]

So, it is not important that the people of the "soul community" be able to theologize with orthodox constructs, but rather that they demonstrate a firm belief in God through their ability to cope with all of life's experiences.[19] Neither is it an issue as to whether the core theological beliefs of the "soul community" are even verbalized. Often either articulated incompletely or left unarticulated, say Cooper-Lewter and Mitchell, core beliefs and foundational attitudes are the operative opinions of the folk about God.[20] In short, a world view that serves as a means of emotional balance is itself a theology.[21]

I was eventually able to push beyond the re-search of Cone and of Cooper-Lewter and Mitchell and discover that the blues were not only religious in the broadest sense of the word, in the Tillichian sense of religion, but that their lyrics revealed blues singers to have drawn directly from the mythologies, theologies, and theodicies of the Judeo-Christian tradition (in a mix with African religious retentions).[22] More specifically, I found that the folk blues are replete with mythologies that reveal blues singers' religious thought on the origin and description of evil, that it is a music that is theological and that talks about evil in folk theological language, and that it is a music that posits "theodicies" reconciling the seeming incongruence of evil existing in a world believed to be created and ruled by a good God. I will return to this latter aspect about blues positing theodicies in the next chapter, when I discuss the blues as a popular music, but only wish to point out at present that Cone insisted that the blues did not attempt to contend with the "problem of evil" and I found him to be incorrect.[23]

It was as a result of my study of the blues that I began to develop the discipline of theomusicology. In fact, it is because theomusicology evolved out of my study of the blues that I have argued that it is the musicological discipline whose re-search is least reductive of the momentousness of black music. In other words, I found that the questions and concerns that arose as I studied the blues were not historical-musicological questions about style periodicy, or ethnomusicological concerns about human behavior or musical skill in music performance. The questions and concerns that arose, to which I gave priority in the development of theory, were not, in other words, historical or social scientific questions and concerns, but indigenous religious questions and concerns—vital questions and ultimate concerns coming directly from the "soul community." The questions that the blues had me ask of them—questions that necessitated the development of a disciplinary perspective that would permit them—derived from the fact that the blues proved not to be "evil," as Cone as well as Cooper-Lewter and Mitchell had figured, but rather characterized by a synthesis of the sacred and the profane. That is to say, the blues were characterized by a synchronous duplicity—the meshing of seeming opposites. This synchronous duplicity made the blues representative of the world view that music scholars, such as ethnomusicologist J. H. Kwabena Nketia, have long acknowledged as typical of black culture. Thus, I began to look at the blues as a paradigm for black cultural criticism and scholarly analysis.

As the "integrative inquiry" being fashioned through the integration of musicology and theology led me to literary study, I found that Houston Baker, Jr., had also taken the blues to be a repository of potential theory for the interpretation and criticism of black culture, particularly that culture's literature.[24] I also found that Henry Louis Gates, Jr., had selected as his repository for an indigenous black literary theory the black trickster known as the Signifying Monkey, who, depersonified and theorized, is the equivalent of the rhetorical artifice of signifying.[25] But through my theomusicological re-search into the blues, I found that Baker's and Gates's sources of indigenous black theory—the blues and the black trickster—are one and the same. That is to say, a direct lineage can be traced from the African tricksters (with whom Gates commences his genealogy toward theory) to the black tricksters whose characters entered the lyrics of the blues (where Baker commences his search for theory), and from there into the personages of blues singers themselves (who emulated the tricky figures they sang about), and onward into the genealogy of black music-makers spawned from the aesthetic of the bluesman paradigm. Briefly I will extrapolate this lineage.

In black folk-heroic literature, trickster personalities were fashioned and refashioned out of the conscious and unconscious needs of blacks to "act bad" and "talk back" in the face of the guardians of the South's slavocracy. The badman figure, whose heritage lays in the African trickster, was one of the tricksters who captured the folk imagination of and became a part of the "folk" or "soul theology" of blacks during the 1890s and beyond because of his uncanny ability to outsmart whites and even the devil. Blacks found in the tradition of the badman, and other figures of wit and guile such as Tar Baby and Brer Rabbit, a means of maintaining emotional balance and a wholesome existence due to the assuagement the trickster provided for their frustrations. Blacks thus saw in the trickster an emulative model of behavior that they transmitted in their trickster tales, ballads, and blues, and later rhythm and blues. So, when badman heroes appeared in the lyrics of the blues, it was generally the blues singer himself, as protagonist in his own songs, who was portrayed as the "baddest." So attractive and cathartic were these self-portrayals that the badman-lives sung about became the badman-lives lived. The folk theology of the trickster and the core theological beliefs or foundational attitudes operative among the folk require story to be intelligible, story or narrative that then becomes a model for lives to be lived. Folklorist John Burrison says the "narrative impulse"—the need to story about or listen to story that structures experiences and imagination into plot—is one of the traits that makes people human,[26] but the "narrative impulse" is also one of the traits that makes people religious.

For example, blues singers who portrayed themselves as divine lovers were embodying the story of the sexually prolific African trickster, who was both malevolent and benevolent, disruptive and reconciliatory, subhuman and superhuman, sexual and spiritual. But as the mythology surrounding the famous country bluesman Robert Johnson illustrates, prolific sexuality and deep spirituality (in his case, spirituality derived from his involvement in voodoo) comprise a synchronous duplicity. Like the black preacher, also of the tradition of the trickster's rhythms, Johnson's singing, often but a protracted moan to which words were attached, was as sexual as it was spiritual. Even if we were speaking of Charlie Patton, Leadbelly, Memphis Minnie, Peetie Wheatstraw, or Rubin Lacy, they all embodied the mythology, lived the story, and could trace their lineage of synchronous duplicity back to the African trickster.

The same is substantially true of the heritage of the black preacher, whom the blues singer had always criticized in self-defense as being no different from himself, particularly when it comes to the love of women. To hear it told in the context of southern jokelore is really to hear it told by the blues singer. In one story, a "colored" preacher called a meeting after his first service at a new church. Using it as an opportunity for himself and the congregation to get to know and understand one another, he asked for everyone who loved the Lord to sit on one side of the church and everyone who loved wine and women to sit on the other side. One man did not budge but looked rather puzzled. When the preacher inquired as to the problem, the man explained that he did not know what side to sit on because he loved the Lord and also loved wine and women. The preacher responded, "Well, son, you jest come up here in de pulpit wi' me. You's been called t' preach."[27]

Humor aside, I believe that the momentousness in

the music that black preachers and blues singers created may be a direct consequence of the synchronous duplicity they embodied. Jung's concept of "the Self"—the archetype of wholeness whose nature it is to unite opposites—offers one possible analogy that is perhaps appropriate, since Jung did work on the trickster figure in American Indian lore and was on a search to comprehend the holistic nature of the cosmos.[28] The archetype of "the Self" requires that human beings integrate into their consciousness all that belongs to its essential wholeness but which the consciousness has rejected and repressed, such as so-called evil.[29] Black music seems to embody the capacity to permit wholeness in black lives due to the fact that black music-makers and music-making contexts naturally blur and even obliterate the boundaries westerners have erected between alleged opposites—the spiritual and the sexual, good and evil, and so forth. To integrate into our consciousness all that belongs to its essential wholeness but which the consciousness has rejected and repressed, permits us, for instance, to appreciate Charlie Spand's most righteous declaration that I quoted in my prologue: "Just as sure as the good Lord sits in the heaven above, now your life ain't all pleasure unless you be with the one you love."

Black music-making contexts that blur and even obliterate the boundaries westerners have created between alleged opposites are contexts that exist in betwixt-and-between spaces of repressively "structured" societies. The "communitas" that breaks in through the cracks of structure in liminality, in at the edges of structure in marginality, from beneath structure in inferiority, and from above structure in spirituality, is what actually blurs or obliterates those boundaries. I surmise that the power that black people are able to generate corporately in those spaces within, beneath, beside, and above suppressive structures of society—those spaces that "the Self" is able to forge out for rhythmic ritual—is the same power that the traditional music-makers of the black folk genres, from the black preacher to the blues singer, were able to glean through embodiment of the trickster personality in the "soul theology."

As my re-search began to disclose this kind of ideation and theory which seemed to provide new insights into and a systematic means of excavating the momentousness of music, it also began to cast revealing light on the limitations of the traditional forms of musicology, which have been accepting of the traditional western boundaries between the alleged opposites. As the allegedly irreligious blues came to be viewed as religious in the new light that my spiritual archaeology had cast upon it, that same light turned upon traditional sacred music revealed that music to be religiously cosmetic, if not in fact religiously ingenuine. Only someone who has lived the blues life, as I preached of the prodigal son in my prologue, can acquiesce the vantage point of privy into the religious process of human maturity. As former blues singer Reverend Rubin Lacy says, church music tended to lack this vantage point:

> The blues is just more truer than a whole lot of the church songs that people sing. Sometimes I think the average person sings a church song just for the tune, not for the words.... But the blues is sung not for the tune. It's sung for the words mostly.... Now you get out here to sing a church song about "When I take my vacation in Heaven." That couldn't be the truth. That's a lie in the church, because a vacation means to go and come. You don't take a vacation in heaven. But now if you're playing the blues, you say "I never missed my water 'til my well went dry." That's the truth.... That's the difference in a church song and the blues.[30]

Thus, traditional sacred music may be doctrinally correct from the perspective of organized religion, but it is not anthropologically, sociologically, or psychologically reflexive of people's religious beliefs and behaviors in the real world. Human beings are not the holy people of moderation that traditional sacred music portrays them as, but are in reality people of extremes—love and hate, peace and war, life and death. If we really want to understand what the masses of black people are thinking religiously, we cannot turn solely (if at all) to the music of institutional religion in which provisional answers to the vital questions and ultimate concerns are already doctrinally predetermined. Divinity scholar Clyde Steckel agrees, saying, "So-called secular music, which seems only or primarily worldly, will disclose depths of feelings and meanings about life in this world which religious music may miss or deny."[31]

As I will demonstrate in the next two chapters, in which I re-search black popular music (chapter 4) and black classical music (chapter 5), we must look to the musics that flourish outside the domains of institutional religion, in places where there is a more candid and authentic religious discourse, no matter how profane those places and discourses may appear to be, no matter how incompletely articulated those core beliefs may seem. If we look to the musics that flourish outside the domains of institutional religion, I believe what we will find will permit us to begin to reconcile those "alleged opposites" I have been speaking of, those aspects of our humanity that are not strange to one another but which have been estranged from one another.

CHAPTER 4

POPULAR MUSE

Although I had come by way of a Christian-theological study of black preaching and the spirituals to this point of being able to apply a broader spiritual archaeology that permits a combing of the religious depths of secular popular music, it was not long before I realized that the social sciences and philosophy—particularly the anthropology, sociology, psychology, and philosophy of music—had a heritage of ideation too rich to ignore. While this ideation is often suggestive of the religious, it is necessary, as I also explained in chapter 2, to exercise caution in borrowing from these disciplines.

For example, some of the traditional questions pondered in the philosophy of music as it has addressed European classical music are not so appropriate for the research of black popular music. This is partly because the philosophy of music, since the European Enlightenment era of Immanuel Kant and Eduard Hanslick, has been dominated by "musical formalism." Akin to Kant's "aesthetic formalism," which emphasizes the structure of art, musical formalism places musical structure (the musical score) at the center of inquiry. This kind of philosophical thought about European classical music is simply unfitting for philosophical discussion about black popular music, for which it is either the live performance or the high-tech recording (rather than the musical score) that is the ideal musical entity.

A philosophy of popular music would doubtless raise some interesting questions worth pondering. Such questions might include whether live-performance lip-synching against studio recordings implies that for popular music the high-tech recording rather than the spontaneous performance is the ideal musical entity, especially since studio overdubbing and splicing are able to perfect music to a degree that the live performance is unable. Samuel Floyd suggests that the live performance is the ideal musical entity, for he sees the value of having a culture-derived approach to black music re-search comprised of a system of referencing drawn from black folk music, a system of referencing which would make audience participation in performances, competitive values, and the intertwining of music and dance into a framework of music criticism in indigenous contexts.[1] In any case, philosophical questions about the ideal musical entity—the high-tech performance versus the live performance—make it clear that a philosophy of popular music, which considers such technology as the LP and CD recording, the music video, and the Walkman radio, would have to differ somewhat from the philosophical discourse that evolved around the discussion of European classical music.

On the other hand, some of the traditional philosophical questions raised with regard to European classical music are directly transferable to our re-search of black popular music, though we might expect different answers. For instance, we certainly could ask the question of questions: What is (popular) music? In the philosophy of popular music this could flush out to be: Where does the existence of popular music commence—prior to composition (musical discoverism), at the point of compositional documentation (musical formalism), or at the point of performance (which we can call musical functionalism)? In other words, is popular music to be defined ontologically, structurally, or sociologically?

For instance, one extreme form of musical formalism is "musical Platonism," which holds that music is an ideal, ontological entity that transcends physical reality and is only imperfectly embodied in the material world via performance. If we listen past scratches on an old recording of a popular blues or correct mistakes in poor performances, would we not be leaning towards musical Platonism and acknowledging some ideal or correct musical entity that precedes the performance of that blues? Or would we not at least be implying the feasibility of a best possible performance of that blues?[2] More specifically, with technology now available to improve older recordings, exactly which recording is the ideal reproduction of that blues—the original LP with its crackling sounds or the cleaned-up CD? This is the same question being debated about old black-and-white movie classics versus technologically colorized versions.

Another traditional question in the philosophy of music that is directly transferable to a philosophy of popular music involves the question of how and through which senses music affects society at large and listeners individually—intellectually, emotionally, or physically. We may also inquire as to whether the way people respond to popular music reveals something about the human psyche and human character in general. Corollary philosophical questions are whether we should talk or write about music in emotional or intellectual terms and whether there should be an ethical dimension to philosophical discourse. If there should be an ethical dimension then what should such an ethics comprise? In the case of discourse on black popular music, should an ethics be especially fitting for black people? These questions and considerations suggest a plausible objective for the integrative re-searcher of black music: to determine what a philosophy of popular music would be and to devise the appropriate discourse.

But I want to stress the view that these are but penultimate questions, penultimate because they fall largely in the realm of thought and reason—David Burrows's "field 2." Because I agree with Paul Tillich that the religious ultimate is presupposed in every philosophical question,[3] I view philosophical questions as mediated questions. That is, philosophical questions are religious questions raised by modern intellectuals of the European Enlightenment heritage who have tried to be areligious (but still give themselves away in terms of a fundamental and inescapable religiosity). This means that for the masses of black people, who make no attempt to deny or camouflage their religiosity or their faith, these philosophical questions are rather synthetic: they are questions that have evolved out of matrices of reason that result from philosophers' prolific thinking. Although the researcher of black music should be cautious in drawing from a discipline that presupposes disbelief in people's concrete religious world views, nevertheless it should be a most fascinating task for the re-searcher first to determine what philosophical discourse is as regards popular music and then to decipher the religious meanings that presuppose and are inherent to that discourse.

But I should also admit that while I think much can be learned from creating a discourse called philosophy of popular music and from reading theologically the mediated questions of that discourse, there is at present no need to give priority to that mediated course (unless one happens to be a philosopher), for we have hardly begun to excavate the vast knowledges that can be uncovered by a direct spiritual archaeology. After all, blues, jazz, rhythm and blues, soul, pop, and rap are forms of black popular music that have their beginning among blacks who gave them recognizable elements of their African-rooted religiosity and rhythmicity. A spiritual archaeology unmediated by philosophy could also pursue the argument I made in chapter 1 about the religious places of ritual for black people (sacred and secular places) being places of religion, such that religion and rhythm are revealed as being one and the same.

The latter pursuit is what we see theomusicologist Angela Nelson engaged in in an essay comparing blues and rap. Nelson discusses her idea that blacks have ascribed to their rhythm a "ritual place" in their spiritual cosmology, a ritual place that implies its sacredness.[4] After showing rhythm and rhyme to be siblings, Nelson cites a rap in which Kool Moe Dee alludes that rhythm and religion are inseparable. Kool Moe Dee says he "floats on his rhymes" to the "level with the gods" and "totes loads and mounds of people to new heights"—to levels of transcendence, interprets Nelson.[5] Philip Royster suggests the same in an essay on rap artist Hammer:

> Hammer employs music and dance in an ethnically and historically determined style in an effort to prompt his community to employ traditions that will enable their spiritual fulfillment, to cross the illusory boundaries of time and space in order to experience the cosmic oneness and inseparableness of all things. This is not merely a logical or conceptual oneness limited to such rational dimensions as doctrine or dogma. It is a spiritual oneness within the womb of cosmic origins, through which wholeness, health, and youth are obtainable. Hence, beneath the masks of the secular black world—masks that often appear profane to some—lie spiritual meanings and behaviors that connect contemporary African Americans to the primordial life force of their African ancestors. Underneath the secular exterior of the popular black musician is an African priest, a shaman, maintaining ancient traditions, opening spiritual doors, and negotiating crossroads through popular culture.[6]

Theomusicologist Mark Sumner Harvey also pursues the inseparability of religion and rhythm:

> It is the rhythmic aspect that bridges all the various styles and approaches now found in popular music, although particular rhythmic feels may vary greatly. I am convinced that more than

melodic or harmonic content, song structure, lyrics, or the latest technological effect, it is rhythm that most profoundly appeals to the popular music listeners. All other aspects are anchored by its solidity, stability, and repetitiveness. It is not enough merely to hear the groove; you must be drawn inside it, and it must penetrate to your inner core. As a line from an old song by The Band put it, "Give me the beat, boys, and fill my soul; I want to get lost in your rock 'n' roll, and drift away."

Furthermore, it is the rhythmic aspect that brings people together. Audiences are drawn together and into the rhythmic pulse that unites them with the performers. Stylized movement and dance choreography among the performers adds yet another dimension and, if audience members are able to dance, this only serves to further intensify the whole experience. It does this by sending the power of the rhythm through the body, energizing and vitalizing all its parts. As Gerardus van der Leeuw noted many years ago, dance and music, but particularly dance and rhythm, constitute the earliest of humankind's ways to the sacred, here construed as connection with elemental power to the ends of ecstasy and participation in a collectivity larger than oneself. This accounts for the importance of constantly having a radio, tape player, or music television station turned on in order to continue this experience.[7]

So, the re-searcher of black music need not give priority to taking the mediated course toward new knowledges by pursuing a philosophy of popular music. Too, the impetus to pursue the most direct course of re-search, "field 3" re-search, can be the estimable goal of reconciling religion and culture via a theology of culture. Or perhaps I should say that the challenge can be to reconcile the sacred and the profane, for it is quite evident that secular black culture (including its popular music) is already understood theologically, as evidenced by the fact that it has always been evaluated with language that pits good against evil. Van der Leeuw generally makes my point when he says that if art is perceived to be demonic then the service of the demonic is also a kind of religion.[8] Divinity scholar Clyde Steckel gets at the same idea differently when he states that even profane or anti-religious music can be understood as people's search for the divine by attempting to envision its opposite.[9] Or we can take German theomusicologist Bernd Schwarze's purview, that since it is a well-known psychological theory that efforts to repress disagreeable experiences do not succeed then it may be that profane music is a place where the problems pushed aside by people in search for the sacred or the holy appear.[10] In other words, human beings already ascribe to a theology of culture, but it is a purview skewed by orthodox doctrine. So, the impetus to pursue a direct spiritual archaeology unmediated by philosophy can be the estimable goal of reconciling the sacred and profane.

What I have just said suggests an ideal methodology for trying to revise our negative unification of religion and culture. First we can illustrate that secular (or profane) black music is already understood from a religious purview. Then we can make arguments, as I do in my prologue, that these negative theological views of secular black music can be revised. This is the methodology I first suggested in *Theological Music: Introduction to Theomusicology,* where I presented three analytical approaches to doing theomusicology: descriptive, normative, and predictive theomusicology. I described *descriptive theomusicology* as involving a nonjudgmental description of the creators and consumers of music, *normative theomusicology* as an analysis of the same in comparison with some source(s) of canonical authority, and *predictive theomusicology* as an analysis of the future state of affairs to which music speaks or directs a society.[11] Philosopher Kathleen Higgins has captured an aspect of what I mean by the latter, the predictive, in her discussion of music as a source of ethical reflection. She says, "Our music gives us a vision of ourselves. In this sense, it can help us understand what we actually value and *where our values are leading us.*"[12]

To illustrate the strategic means by which the theomusicologist can help reconcile the sacred and profane, I will utilize descriptive and normative theomusicology. My descriptive theomusicology will comprise my nonjudgmental description of how people, who have not yet reconciled the sacred and profane in their religious doctrine, already conceive of secular black music in theological terms (albeit negatively). With regard to the second phase of analysis—normative theomusicology—the black community generally gauges the normative by the canonical authority of the Bible as it has been traditionally (albeit variously) interpreted by the black church. The descriptive phase, which I will commence in a moment, is simple enough to understand, but I should say more about the normative phase of analysis before I begin.

As I said, it is the black church's guardianship of biblical interpretation that is an essential source of black cultural normativity. We see this normativity expressed in the work of Christian theomusicologists N. Lynne Westfield and Harold Dean Trulear in their essay on rap artist Hammer. Westfield and Trulear say, "we will argue that the music of Hammer points to a form of spirituality that is inconsistent with historic African American spiritual norms, that it substitutes an inadequate form of self-transcendence for true knowledge of God, and that it does not provide the communal base of identity necessary for meaningful life and wholeness."[13] But as theomusicologists, Westfield and Trulear know that to accept the implications of their spiritual archaeology, acceptance dependent on the exercise of "hermeneutical control" over the Bible, is to recognize that there are also other sources of canonical authority which they are obliged to consider in any project of assessing black cultural traditions. My prologue alludes that the normativity that I think broadens that of the black church, which doctrinally accepts the estrangement of religion and culture learned from the white church, is the canonical authority of the black trickster and a theology of the crossroads. Though Westfield and Trulear ultimately have in mind the spiritual norms of the black church, they exemplify the fact that these norms perhaps need only to be broadened rather than displaced. They say:

> Theomusicology, for us, becomes a discipline that encourages the investigation of the process of socialization as a fundamentally religious or theological one, whether the data in question is secular music or traditional church music. Theomusicology treats black life in a holistic manner and secularity as a context for the sacred and profane rather than as the antithesis of the sacred. The historic values and traditions of African American life are the context for the evaluation of all socialization, whether it be the music of rappers or the gospel chorus. In asserting its concern for secular music, theomusicology argues for a fundamentally religious understanding of the whole of life and enables us to assess the music of rap artists as a form of "religious education" (if by "religion" we refer to the realm of the transcendent and its ethical dimensions). As such, theomusicology is a tool for us to move beyond the simplistic notions of "good" and "bad" that are uncritically used to categorize black secular music and especially rap music, and to help us develop an understanding of the meaning system under construction by African American youths and gain stronger insight into their needs.[14]

So, to illustrate how the theomusicologist can help reconcile the sacred and profane, I will employ descriptive and normative theomusicology, and my source of normativity will be the canonical authority of the trickster and a theology of the crossroads, which result from my taking hermeneutical control over that traditional source of black cultural normativity—the Bible. I will begin with descriptive theomusicology, which will reveal how secular black popular music is already viewed religiously as demonic, but then through my normative theomusicology how we can (still viewing it religiously) interpret it as not demonic but as fulfilling and in some respects salvational. If I am successful at this then I will have prepared the way, along with what I will do in the next chapter on classical music, for our spiritual archaeology to excavate an ethics that is indigenous to black culture. If I am able to accomplish this, then I will have set up a permanent alternative source of canonical authority for black cultural analysis, an alternative source that does not so much displace as it does broaden that canonical authority under the guardianship of the black church.

I will begin my descriptive theomusicology by documenting religious views of the blues that have resulted from the old source of canonical authority. But let me say again that descriptive theomusicology simply describes without interpretive interference. So, in the following pages I will describe how black secular music, from blues to rap, has been viewed as demonic. Then, and only then, as promised, I will proceed to do normative theomusicology. At that point, to reemphasize the point, we will look through the very same theological lens that has doubted the religious nature of these musics and refocus that lens to see what we will then see. At that point I will respond to the negative theological critiques of all the genres of secular music and especially the heavy allegations made against the music and person of Prince. Now I will commence my descriptive theomusicology, which will show how secular black popular music is already viewed religiously as demonic.

When the blues first began to develop as a commercial art form during the early 1920s, it was viewed as profane and evil not only by whites but by blacks, and not only by poor blacks of the rural South but by middle-class blacks of the urban North. In both the rural South and the urban North this view of blues as "evil" was due to the imposition of the western world view which insisted upon the separation of religion and culture and the demonization of the latter. In the urban North, among a growing educated class of blacks, we might least expect to hear talk about blues being evil; but this was not the case. For example, Lucius Harper, a black journalist for *The Chicago Defender*, wrote in an article of the late 1930s, titled

"We Prefer the 'Blues' to Our Essential Causes," that while blacks have failed in the fundamental cause of gleaning political recognition from whites, they have succeeded in winning favor and almost unanimous popularity for their blues songs and "jitterbug accomplishments." He wrote, "Our blue melodies have been made popular because they are different, humorous and silly. The sillier the better. They excite the primitive emotion in man and arouse his bestiality. He begins to hum, moan and jump usually when they are put into action. They stir up the emotions and fit in handily with bootleg liquor. They break the serious strain of life and inspire the "on with the dance" philosophy. They are popular because the American people, both white and black, relish nonsense."[15]

Indeed, the church had taught this very thing about the world outside its sacred enclave: it was a world of bootleg liquor and an "on with the dance" philosophy. The hymnody of the era, for instance the gospel hymns of Charles Price Jones and Charles Albert Tindley, reflected this anticulturalism. The songs of Jones consider the "traditions of men" to be "unworthy of authority,"[16] and they depict the world as an evil realm wherein "ev'ry trusted friend forsake[s]," "kindred drive thee from their door," "thou art despised and lone," and "none will speak a word of cheer." Life, Jones lyricizes, is an "open sea" swept over by "raging storms of sore affliction," and those who ascribe to its ways are woefully wicked.[17] Tindley, like Jones, complains in his gospel hymns that the human domain is a "world of sin" and "world of tears," a "wilderness" from which, he writes, "I shall be free some day." Whereas Jones tends to generalize about the spiritual transgression of the world, Tindley typically specifies social aspects of its decadence.[18]

Jazz fared no better than the blues in this kind of dialectic or polemic with church music. Throughout the 1920s, debate raged among whites regarding whether this music of an allegedly inferior race had intoxicating power that could cause sexual promiscuity and interracial mixing. Thus, blacks became just as concerned about jazz becoming, in the words of black columnist Alexander Jackson, the "new and terrible standard of blues and morals" capable of stunting spiritual growth.[19] Robert Abbott, the founder and editor of *The Chicago Defender*, also disapproved of this music and the dance halls, cabarets, and underground taverns he believed to be scandalizing the morals of black youths: "Our sedate young ladies..., tearing down every conceivable hope of redemption, abandon themselves into such frenzied, epileptic contortions as 'snake-hip,' 'black-bottom' and the vulgar dance de ventre, known as the 'rhumba,' to the tune of 'Shake That Thing.'"[20] Elliott Rawlins, a medical doctor who wrote a column titled "Keeping Fit" for *The New York Amsterdam News* during the 1920s, went so far as to apply a medical hermeneutic to this discourse, but one still visibly laced with religious concern:

> From time immemorial, the fact has been known that music has an effect upon the brain. Music can soothe and music can stimulate. Music has made you cry, and music has made you laugh. In the same way music can bring you into a reflective mood, in which the mind ponders, thinks and reasons. By the same process music may overstimulate, confuse and finally paralyze the thinking and reasoning center of the brain, and leave you intoxicated and drugged. This latter effect is the predominating result of jazz music. In these days of prohibition, it frequently takes the place of whiskey, wine and beer.
> The Brain can be affected through stimulation from the internal metabolism of the body. Such a result is noted after eating or drinking. The impression reaches the brain by absorption of the chemical and physiological products from the stomach and the intestines, and these getting into the circulating blood stimulates the brain as it passes through its delicate cells. Such a result occurs after drinking whiskey or other alcoholic liquors.
> The Brain can also be affected by impressions and stimulations reaching it through the sense of touch and sight; the sense of smelling and the sense of hearing; many persons have fainted, and some have died suddenly by seeing a serious accident. . . .

> Bracing music of a quick and stimulating tempo is played to urge the soldiers as they march to war; sacraments of the church are accompanied by soft, sweet, plaintive or solemn music to aid the worshippers to spiritual thoughts. All through life, impressions and stimulations are given to the brain through the medium of the senses.
> Thus the quick and staccato tempo of jazz music, with the plaintive and pleading notes of the violin and clarinet; the screeching of the horns; the moaning of the trombone; the calling and imploring tones of the saxophone; the rhythmic beating of the drums, all these send a continuous whirl of impressionable stimulation to the brain producing thoughts and imaginations which overpower the will. Reason and reflection are lost, and the actions of the person are directed by the stronger animal passions.
> In other words, jazz music intoxicates; it affects the brain through the sense of hearing, giving the same results as whiskey or other alcoholic drinks taken into the system by way of the stomach. It has the same effect as a drug and one may become addicted to its use. The more you hear it the more you desire its stimulation.
> In the social life of the people today jazz music is king, and jazz music will reign until a spiritual awakening reformation sweeps like a whirlwind over the land. . . .
> The human brain always reacts to the strongest impressions received. To overcome the effect of jazz music, one has to have knowledge of its harmful results, and the reflecting and sobering impressions of life's experience. To the young and inexperienced jazz music is dangerous.[21]

Two years later Rawlins published the same article but added an introductory paragraph that equated the intoxication of jazz with that of the opiate. He began, "Morphine, cocaine and opium are powerful drugs which can be used for relief of pain. They are used only in this legitimate way by the guidance of a physician, for a definite purpose only. In any other way they are useless and harmful, and their sale and use are specifically determined by law. This is not so with jazz. The form of music called jazz is just as intoxicating as morphine or cocaine; it is just as harmful, and yet its use is not determined by law."[22]

This kind of negative religious hermeneutic applied to secular black popular music did not cease when the "quick and staccato tempo of jazz" cooled down during the 1940s into the new genre of black popular music known as rhythm and blues. This new music was comprised of a synthesis of blues, gospel, and small and big band swing—a mix modernized by the incorporation of the new technology of the electric bass. But rhythm and blues was not simply a fusion of blues, jazz, and gospel styles, all undergirded by the meta-style of black rhythm. Ray Charles's rhythm-and-blues song titled "Hallelujah, I Love Her So" exemplifies that it was no less than what Cornel West called the "spiritual-blues impulse"—a synthesis of worldly secularity and black church spirituality: the word "Hallelujah" belongs to the church and the words "I Love Her So" belong to the world. What Ray Charles did, as did other rhythm-and-blues performers like Dave Clark, King Curtis, Otis Redding, Sam Cooke, Aretha Franklin, and James Brown, was to obliterate the Victorian partition between the sacred and the profane by bluesifying black religion and black-religionizing the blues. This synthesis of the sacred and the profane, this synchronous duplicity (that existed in practice but not in theory in black culture), was such that many former gospel singers were severely reprimanded by black preachers and church members for being lured into the nightclubs and for carrying their church dramaturgy into the profane context. Like its secular musical predecessors—blues and jazz—rhythm and blues was understood to be unreligious, in part because the world in which it flourished was considered, as Thomas Dorsey described it in his gospel music of this era, a "world of sin" full of despair and heavy burdens, sorrow and troubles, earthly trials, and battles with foes pressing in on every side.[23]

With blacks making substantial gains in their quality of life during the final quarter of the twentieth century, gospel music has not been as anticultural as in times past. Thus, the cleavage between gospel and soul music began to close when the Edwin Hawkins Singers recorded the modern arrangement of the old Baptist hymn "O Happy Day" in 1969. However, another kind of criticism came to bear on soul music when rhythm and blues of the 1940s and 1950s was reincarnated. Leonard Barrett, writing in the early 1970s, attempted to distinguish between real and counterfeit "soul" by calling soul music ingenuine. He said that real "soul" is the moral and emotional substance that has sustained black people through a history of adverse conditions, but that the term "soul" had become so popularized that it lost its potency and genuineness: "'Soul' is a germinal idea, born out of deep social conflict; yet all such ideas seem to spin off into ridiculousness, to take on broad and vogue connotations and the term 'soul' is no exception. Thus in advertising parlance we now have 'soul music,' all kinds of jungle rhythms, not necessarily African. . . . However, in order not to appear left out, the wider society uses the word, but only for form's sake and certainly without tuning in on the 'peculiar' feeling that properly defines it."[24]

The music of the contemporary performers of black pop has also received negative religious criticism, as exemplified in the responses to a news release announcing the theomusicology conference I held April 7–8, 1989, on the theme "The Theology of American Popular Music." Held at Duke Divinity school in the little chapel in which the school's worship is held three days a week, lectures were given on Thelonious Monk, James Brown, Marvin Gaye, Stevie Wonder, Michael Jackson, Al Green, Prince, and Run-D.M.C. (all males due to the choice of the female and male lecturers to write on these figures). In response to my statement in the news release that Prince was a "preacher" of sorts who posited his own brand of theology, that Prince is clearly someone who is religious and spiritual and yet highlights what it means to be also carnal,[25] the editors of *The United Methodist Reporter,* a church newspaper, responded angrily:

> To begin with, calling Prince a "preacher" implicitly insults countless genuine preachers of the Gospel. He isn't a preacher. He's a shameless entertainer who sells his music by exploiting the most base human instincts. Furthermore, it's "straining at a gnat" to suggest that Prince's music is worth listening to because something resembling religion is buried in the filth. Come on. We're not talking the "pearl of great price" here. It's simply poor stewardship to expend time and energy sorting through the garbage for Prince's alleged spiritual nuggets. Finally, why exalt Prince as one who "embodies the contradictions of being human?" Who doesn't? Part of our flawed nature as sinful human beings is our "contradictions"—our inconsistency and inconstancy in being faithful to God. We don't need Prince as a reminder of that truth. We can just look at "the man in the mirror," as a popular Michael Jackson song points out. It's a good idea for us as Christians to glean from popular culture insights into the nature and will of God. . . . It's a bad idea, however, to abandon our critical faculties in the gleaning process. We shouldn't naively assume we can search in muck for truth and not get soiled. Parts of our culture are just that—muck—and we should have enough courage of our convictions to say so.[26]

I will respond to these allegations in a moment, for at the moment I am still in my mode of descriptive theomusicology, which is intended to show that secular black popular music is already viewed religiously, albeit as demonic. Before I respond to these allegations I first want to show, finally, that the detractors of rap have been just as ultimately concerned, some going so far as to equate rap with rape. This equation is first seen in Tipper Gore's *Washington Post* editorial titled "Hate, Rape and Rap,"[27] the juxtaposition of *rape* and *rap* evident in the title alone. This equation again occurs in a *Newsweek* editorial titled "America's Slide into the Sewer" by journalist George Will, in which the rap lyrics of 2 Live Crew are juxtaposed with explicit testimonies of the legal defendants regarding the alleged rape of a female jogger in New York's Central Park in April 1990.[28] Then in *USA Today* it was reported that during sentencing one of the males convicted in this case "swaggered through a rambling, rap-styled poem he had composed in jail."[29] To go further, on the *CBS Evening News with Dan Rather*, on August 22, 1991, a journalist doing a piece on serial killers, with brief clips of serial killers ranging from Son of Sam to Jeffrey Dahmer, mentioned rap in the context of discussing the country's problems of hate and violence and showed a clip of rapper Ice T.

This completes my descriptive theomusicology which, over the last several pages, has intended to demonstrate that people already apply a religious hermeneutic to their understanding of secular black popular music. Now let us move on to normative theomusicology and look through the very same theological lens to see what we will see if we refocus it by doing as Westfield and Trulear did in their analysis of Hammer—taking "hermeneutical control" over and broadening our interpretation of that principal canonical source of the black community. I intentionally refrained from defending my view that secular black popular music is theological in a positive way, but let us now return to the beginning of our heritage of secular black popular music, starting with the blues, and I will make my case. But let us remember what Christian theomusicologists Westfield and Trulear said: that theomusicology encourages the treatment of black life in "a holistic manner" and secularity as "a context for the sacred and profane rather than as the antithesis of the sacred."[30] As I go back over this heritage of secular black popular music with a refocused lens, I will summarize the re-search done by the speakers at the theomusicology conference I hosted at Duke Divinity School in 1989.[31] Included in my summary of these lectures will also be my delayed response to the harsh words about the music and demeanor of Prince. But first I will start with the blues.

My own conference talk on the blues was titled "God in Secular Music Culture: The Theodicy of the Blues as the Paradigm of Proof." My intent in that essay was to demonstrate that the early blues singers of the pre–World War II era reflected on both the cause of evil and the nature of suffering just like church folk. I proposed that if I could show that the blues posits theodicies—explanations for the existence of evil and suffering in a world created by an all-knowing, all-powerful, and all-present good-God—then it should be a short step to showing that the secular offspring of the blues (jazz, rhythm and blues, soul, pop, and rap) also possess religious meaning.[32] The principal theodicies of the blues that I discussed were the biblical "reap what you sow" and "work of the devil" theodices, the former being the most typical. Robert Wilkins (who later became a preacher, as many early ex-blues singers did) reflected on the "reap" theodicy in his "Dirty Deal Blues." He sang, "Oh baby I'm glad that this whole round world do know, that every living creature reap just what they sow." I could go on with numerous examples, but these are well documented in my book *Blues and Evil*.

If blues is indeed the paradigm of proof that black secular music is religious, then a consistent theomusicological method would expect the blues's first-born secular offspring also to manifest this. The difficulty in making such a determination about jazz lies in the fact that most of this music is instrumental rather than vocal. This fact made it particularly difficult for Hugh Roberts to discern in jazz what he sensed to be an inherent religiosity. He gave it an attempt in his conference paper on Thelonious Monk, titled "Improvisation, Individuation, and Immanence." Roberts borrowed C. G. Jung's notion of "individuation" to attempt a disclosure of what he sensed to be a secular spirituality in Monk's persona and music. According to his reading of Jung, individuation is a spiritual journey that commences with departure from conformity to church and societal conventions. Akin to the typical blues and jazz musician before him, Roberts said, Monk's spiritual journey began in the church and veered off into the jazz world wherein he was ordained the "High Priest of Bop": "In theological terms *individuation* is the death of (conscious) self and rebirth of the whole person who becomes the expression of God's Will (Romans 6). In the theological lingo of the secular world it is one's 'spiritual journey,' while in the language of the black blues community it is 'jazz.' 'Jazz,' says Martin Williams, 'exalts the individual finding his own way.... Jazz is the music of a people who have been told by their circumstances they are unworthy. And in jazz, these people discover their own worthiness . . . from within.'"[33] Jazz's individuational essence, continued Roberts, is improvisation, which is a kind of spontaneous individuation. Evidenced in part by his unique style of improvising,[34] Monk's individuation was both worshipful and revealing of the immanence of God in the religion of jazz: "Thelonious Monk lived the outward life of a secular jazz musician. But his 'spiritual journey'—his individuation—served as evidence of the immanence of God in his life and music. Religion is of no great importance when it is only a matter of prayer and liturgical ritual. But when it is a principle pervading all life, the sacred and the secular, offering to the immanent God *all* spiritual, sacrificial, and individuational aspects of daily life as continual worship—including the improvisational performance of jazz—that religion is the ideal of humanity."[35]

While Thelonious Monk will always be remembered as the "High Priest of Bop," soul singer James Brown will always be touted as the "Godfather of Soul." Like Monk, Brown was raised in the black church. But unlike Monk's individuational style, Brown's manner and technique was imitative of the oratory and dramaturgy of the black preacher. Earlston DeSilva, in his conference talk on Brown, "The Theology of Black Power and Black Song," called Brown "the most charismatic preacher of the secular world that black folk had ever witnessed."[36] Brown's message of soul, continued DeSilva, was a vital evangelistic means of awakening black youth to the exigency of black power and to the core religious beliefs of the black church that underpinned the black power socio-economic philosophy.[37] He said, "Brown's music also helped unchurched brothers and sisters to rediscover black religion, which overflowed from the church into the secular Soul community, and to rediscover the core religious beliefs of the church, which helped constitute the community's natural religious law."[38]

Complementing DeSilva's defining of the theology of soul was Alton B. Pollard III's conference talk on Al Green, titled "The Last Soul Singer in America." Pollard identified soul music as the offspring of spirituals, hymns, blues, and gospel, all genres he defined as "the musical fruits of a segregated American society, songs of honesty, truth, and anguish, profoundly soul-searching and soul-baring evocations." He continued, "Soul music must to a significant degree be recognized as a continuance of this tradition, as the ongoing working out of African-American folk aspirations, only now with a new functionality born of wider social, political, and economic prospects."[39]

One of the differences between Al Green and James Brown is that Green completed the cycle of departure from and return to the church, a cycle that, as my prologue discussed, was typical of the early blues singers. Raised in the church as a singer in his father's gospel ensemble, Green crossed over to soul music, only to return eventually to the church a gospel singer and preacher. Pollard examined each of these phases, noting particularly Green's "conversional period" when he performed both soul and gospel on the same record album. But ultimately, as Pollard concluded, Green returned to his birthright: "Al Green, the last of the great soul singers has, like the Prodigal Son, been to the far country and is now returned home."[40]

One soul singer who never had the opportunity to return "home" to the church was Marvin Gaye. He was shot to death in 1984 by his own father, a preacher. In her talk titled "The Theology of Sexual Healing," Orea Jones briefly recounted the spirit of social activism in Gaye's *What's Going On* album (1971)—his concern over war, poverty, unemployment, and ecological pollution. But Jones also recognized the antithetical extreme to which Gaye's attention frequently oscillated, an extreme epitomized by his song "Sanctified Pussy" (posthumously modified in title and text to "Sanctified Lady"). Jones said of the original song, "Gaye's oxymoron—his synthesis of the extremes that 'sanctification' and 'pussy' signify—was the precursor of the theme of 'sex as salvation' in the music of Prince."[41] By using Gaye's hit song "Sexual Healing" as a window into America's ethos of eros, Jones found a possible religious motif cryptically tucked away within the song's carnal sensuousness. "It is possible," she contended, "that the notion of 'sexual healing' at *midnight* is somehow derived from symbols gleaned from his religious background, namely that in the sullen quiet of the midnight hour, when life seems darkest, relief comes, the prison gates burst open."[42]

The notion of "sex as salvation" (or at least as liberation) is embraced and continued in the music of Prince, as Richard Wimberley recognized in his conference talk titled "Prophecy, Eroticism, and Apocalypticism in Popular Music." Here is the long-awaited response to the earlier criticisms of Prince in *The United Methodist Reporter,* in which it was said that considering Prince a preacher of sorts was flatly wrong. In his conference lecture Wimberley made no attempt to locate a motif of religiosity in Prince's eroticism, but simply noted that Prince's thematization of eroticism appears adjacent themes of social commentary that denounce such threatening aspects of life as racism, poverty, suicide, AIDS, gang warfare, and even nuclear war. This potpourri of ultimate concern and concern for sexual pleasure Wimberley found symbolized in the photo of Prince on the cover of one of his albums. Wimberley said, "The sacred symbol of the Christian cross breaking his nudity on the cover of *Lovesexy* results in a strange juxtaposition of spirituality and carnality, innocence and pornography, and their synthesis—'sex as salvation.'"[43] Complementing what Wimberley has recognized, Pollard commented thus in his conference lecture on Prince, "Religion, Rock, and Eroticism." His remark is my response to the statement in *The United Methodist Reporter* that Prince's embodiment of "the contradictions of being human" is of no religious significance. Pollard says:

> The haunting physical presence and music of Prince are one. Like religion itself, he is mysterious and anomalous. His existence straddles the margins of the acceptable, where he lives dangerously and behaves outrageously. He is not confined to conventional lifestyles because he symbolizes a power that is, in the language of religion, both mana (attracting, invitive) and taboo (repelling, prohibitive). In fine, Prince is a striking example of the androgynous individual—binary opposites in one, a whole composed of two. It comes as no surprise then that he is esteemed by some as an interpreter of life's ambivalences and ambiguities, mediating between sacred and profane, God and human, eternal and natural, female and male, life and death.[44]

This is not quite the response that will satisfy an evangelical Christian, but it wholly fits within the framework of Paul Tillich's theology of culture, which is at the base of the theomusicology I espouse.

To continue, in comparison to the music of Prince, the music of Stevie Wonder and Michael Jackson is perhaps not at all controversial. Harold Dean Trulear discussed the music of Stevie Wonder in his conference talk titled "The Prophetic Character of Black Secular Music" and Michael Eric Dyson the music of Michael Jackson in his talk titled "A Postmodern Afro-American Secular

Spirituality." Trulear identified Wonder's three-tiered "egalitarian ethics" as a concern for (1) interpersonal love (husband/wife, parents/children, boyfriend/girlfriend), (2) love between the races, and (3) the love of justice. He concluded that, "Stevie Wonder is accentuating themes which have their root in a culture that, while not explicitly Christian, certainly is beholden to a form of ethical monotheism that blends the Judeo-Christian tradition and West-African thought forms."[45] Dyson complemented Trulear's explanation of Wonder's "egalitarian ethics" by pointing out that the ethical and the spiritual in Jackson's music are manifested as religious sensibility to human nature, the nature of good and evil, racial identity and consciousness, the potentiality of self-transformation, and the exigency of peace, love, and justice in the process of human betterment.[46]

Dyson's goal was to examine Jackson's secular spirituality as theatricalized in the media of television and video. Harking back to Hugh Roberts's suggestion that part of Thelonious Monk's spirituality was derived through a process of individuation, Dyson similarly concluded that a crucial aspect of Jackson's theatricalization of spirituality is his traversing of traditional boundaries that categorize and define differences—innocent/shrewd, young/old, black/white, male/female, and religious/secular.[47] Dyson added that: "Jackson's spirituality is secular because it is created for and best thrives in the cultural, psychic, and social spaces of the concert world, and not the *ekklessia*. It is not situated in or sustained by conventional procedures of church participation, service, or worship. This does not mean, however, that Jackson's spirituality is devoid of religious drama involving rituals, pageantry, and spectacles. On the contrary, his secular spirituality, particularly as performed on the concert stage, is replete with references to certain Afro-American religio-cultural practices that signify in the musical arena."[48]

The same thing can be said of rap, which is just as revealing of ultimate concern as the aforementioned forms of music lectured on at the Duke theomusicology conference. The kind of contending with the vital questions that we see in rap is what I like to describe as a quest for salvational knowledge. A spiritual archaeology reveals that rappers posit existential knowledge they believe to be the means by which the most oppressed people of the black community can be "saved" from racial genocide and uplifted politically and economically. These particular rappers posit salient messages that address issues such as drug abuse, black-on-black crime, police-on-black civil terrorism, sexually transmitted disease, teenage pregnancy, women's rights, world peace, and the urgency of education.

With this said, I return reinforced to the ethics suggested in my prologue. First of all, there are people who seem to look to secular black popular music in order to get in touch with the evil that is really in themselves, evil in themselves that is denied by their religious doctrine and suppressed psychologically. Secondly, to be able to enjoy not only sacred music but secular music as well is to be able to be truer to our humanness. With this ethic again in mind, I will draw this chapter to a close with that most righteous passage from Charlie Spand's "Back to the Woods Blues" quoted in my prologue: "Just as sure as the good Lord sits in the heaven above, now your life ain't all pleasure unless you be with that one you love."

CHAPTER 5

CLASSICAL MUSE

Given the western way of thinking derivative of the European Enlightenment, thinking which presupposes a bifurcation of life's unity into the sacred and profane or into religion and culture, it is no wonder the philosophy of music moved into the void created by the unwillingness of musicologists to do theology on culture. How else could an attempt be made to explain the momentousness of the music of their great classical traditions emerging around 1750 since ideas about religion and spirituality were now intellectually outmoded? This suppression of a theological understanding of music was widely accepted by the white American musical establishment, but it was never really manifest among the black composers who worked within the western classical idioms. This is something the white patrons and critics of black classical music misunderstood when this genre of black music began to emerge rapidly during the Negro Renaissance that commenced in the 1920s. Using the classical music of William Grant Still, I will demonstrate what other worlds and realities we can uncover when black music is re-searched with a spiritual archaeology that combs the terrain of "field 3." I have chosen Still not only because he is the best-known black composer of classical music in American history but because he kept an extensive paper trail revealing his spiritual inclinations and their relationship to his art.

Let us commence by exploring what I just called the

"western way of thinking," which I said presupposes a bifurcation of life's unity into the sacred and profane and into religion and culture. Those who accepted this way of thinking often believed that it was only primitive human beings who conceived of religion and culture as a unity, that these primitive peoples simply did not recognize the real opposition between the sacred and the profane. As a consequence, it is only the folk culture of the civilized world, with its traces of the "primitive," that these westerners viewed as religiously authentic. For instance, while Gerardus van der Leeuw is pleased that this cleavage between religion and culture healed somewhat via the recognition of modern humanity that God created not only the human soul but also the body, and while pleased that the "cult of the body" predominant in America has led to the possibility that human beings might gradually reconquer their capacity to express themselves through bodily movement or dance, he still holds that except in folk art human beings are far removed from their primordial holism.[1]

Van der Leeuw's fear of the eternal loss of this primordial unity and his longing for its return in European culture was widespread among white intellectuals in Europe and America during the early twentieth century. In America we see this fear and longing among the white patrons of the Negro Renaissance, Charlotte Osgood Mason and Albert C. Barnes prominent among them. Mason's concern was first manifested in the support she gave folklorist Natalie Curtis, whose research resulted in the publication of *The Indians' Book* (1907), a collection of songs, stories, and drawings that claim to reflect the inner life and soul of one of the noblest types of primitive people.[2] *The Indians' Book* in turn became Mason's bible, to the degree that both its substance and the philosophy behind Curtis's ethnography became part of Mason's own cosmology when she emerged during the late 1920s and early 1930s to become one of the most influential patrons of the black arts. The teachings Mason passed on to the Negro Renaissance artists and intellectuals, including Zora Neale Hurston, Langston Hughes, and Alain Locke, were anticipated two decades earlier in Curtis's introduction to *The Indians' Book*, which says that Anglo-Saxons are a race of people with mechanical and inventive genius but who lack the spontaneous creative impulse of primitive peoples who possess the potential to revive the culture of American civilization. "The primitive races are the child races," Curtis writes. "Who can tell us what may be their contribution to humanity when they are grown? And have they not even now something to give?"[3]

Although Locke was the Negro Renaissance intellectual to whom Mason most often preached this gospel beginning in the late 1920s until she died in the early 1940s, and although Mason had frequently told Locke stories from *The Indians' Book* and eventually gave him an autographed copy, the Harvard-trained philosopher was already familiar with this Enlightenment thought. These ideas certainly undergirded the social sciences and philosophy he studied at Harvard, but similar ideas were also expressed in that crucial work of the Negro Renaissance that he compiled in 1925—*The New Negro*. In the essay titled "Negro Art in America," an article second only to Locke's introductory title-essay, philanthropist Albert C. Barnes wrote that the primitive Negro race, with its folk art unharnessed by the white man's education and pseudo-culture which stifle the soul, can be of tremendous civilizing value to America by helping whites return to their original spiritual endowment—the unity of religion and culture (art). Barnes believed that the spiritual endowment possessed by the primitive Negro race was a source of primeval happiness from which whites had been estranged due to their permitting the mind to dominate over the spirit.[4]

Like Barnes, Mason believed Anglo-Saxon culture was depleted of divine essence, that their white culture "sucks the life blood out of the soul of art that is being born in western civilization."[5] Negroes, they both believed, had not yet lost that "life blood" and could nurture it back to full life if they would only be true to their "primitive" impulses in their art. To Mason, the route to this recovery of their "primitive" authenticity would require Negroes to relinquish their adulterated sexual impulses that whites violently imposed upon them during slavery and to recapture those impulses derived from the primordial unity of the sexual and the spiritual, which so powerfully connected them with God.[6] This is the "original Negro quality" that Mason saw in such Negro folk art as the blues, of which she owned numerous recordings,[7] and which she also saw burgeoning in Langston Hughes's and Claude McKay's writing, in Paul Robeson's and Marian Anderson's concert renditions of the spirituals, and in William Grant Still's classical compositions thematically built upon black folk and popular music.

Langston Hughes eventually wised up and broke with Mason, probably for more reasons than he acknowledged or understood. Mason wanted Hughes to know and feel the intuitions of the primitive, but he discovered that he could not live and write as though he did know and feel these intuitions. "I was only an American Negro—who had loved the surface of Africa and the rhythms of Africa—but I was not Africa," he wrote. "I was Chicago and Kansas City and Broadway and Harlem. And I was not what she wanted me to be."[8] It was not really that Hughes's art or his conception of art, once free of Mason's overlordship, could then return to maintaining the European bifurcation between religion and culture (art), it is simply that Hughes could not be what Mason wanted him to be. In actuality, with regard to what I argued in chapter 1, Hughes's love of the rhythms of Africa was no mere love of the "surface" of Africa. In that chapter I quoted Locke as saying, "This racial mastery of rhythm is one characteristic that seems never to have been lost."[9] Indeed, all of the aforementioned Negro Renaissance artists, though obsessed with mastering the artistic forms of European culture, nonetheless maintained the meta-style of black art that I identified in chapter 1 as being African rhythm.

Along with the white philanthropists of the Negro Renaissance, the white art critics also failed to understand that this meta-style of black art was evidence of a primordial unity of religion and culture, a unity which black schooling in white conservatories of music and which black use of European musical forms did not destroy. The lack of this understanding is seen in the music reviews of Olin Downes, a long-time critic for *The New York Times*. For example, when R. Nathaniel Dett's Hampton Institute choir performed at Carnegie Hall in April of 1928, Downes insisted that the "real" Negro had been eclipsed by white musical influences, that interpretation "more racial in quality" would have been ideal.[10] Revealing his racialist theories about the Negro, Downes continued: "The negro's musical impulses are not those of the white. He is less restrained, and often more individual as well as spontaneous in his expression." Then Downes proceeded to theorize about the "real" spirituals: "Some negro spirituals are wildly dramatic. Often they have rhythms and phrase lengths which cut entirely free from white tradition. Many of them are rollicking rather than pathetic or tragic in expression." Since the spirituals that the Hampton choir rendered were not of Downes's "real" kind, since they were not primitive enough, he then said of the choir's performance: "Could not certain of the harmonizations have been less formal, more exotic? For us there was too much evidence of the musical influence of the whites and not enough of the originality of the race which has given America the spirituals and the dance rhythms that have gone over the whole world."[11]

Downes gave a similar assessment of Dett's *The Ordering of Moses*, an oratorio that tells the biblical story of the Israelites' passage through the Red Sea using the spiritual "Go Down, Moses" as the musical and textual thematic material. Downes had to note the exceptional accomplishments of Dett's career, the success of the oratorio's performance, and the audience's warm reception of the composition, but he still had to assert his belief that Dett's music was insufficiently Negroid:

> Mr. Dett had reason to congratulate himself upon the effect of his music. It was carefully performed, though it must be said that... a wilder and more emotional treatment could have been given certain of the solos and recitatives done in the pale white fashion. And possibly for this reason, and despite the popular reaction, it seems to the present chronicler that while Mr. Dett has done well, he has not gone nearly far enough in striking the racial note in his music....
>
> There is a deeper, greater and more powerful thing, in this same direction, for the Negro artist to do. There is still the question of the way which he is to find to do it, which cannot be the way of either imitation or emulation of another race's culture. "The Ordering of Moses," in so far as it was the expression of a Negro musician, triumphed. The weaknesses are those of a musician educated too well in a conventionalized mold.[12]

Downes had similarly criticized performances of William Grant Still's music, but he found his *Sahdji*, a ballet based on an African story, to be moving in what he considered to be the right direction. He concluded, "It is not Negro music diluted with conventions of the white, nor yet is it cast in the forms of negroid expression which has also become conventional. Mr. Still does not indulge in Harlem jazz, but harks back to more primitive sources for brutal, persistent and barbaric rhythms."[13]

Unable to recognize the unity of religion and culture in black classical music, a unity that was already present without black composers having to strain for the exotic or the primitive, historical musicologists were no more insightful than the music critics and philanthropists who took an interest in Negro Renaissance art. Historical musicologists approached the study of black classical music (in those few instances that attention was even given it) in the same way they went about the study of European classical music—that is, assuming the bifurcation of religion and culture and therefore leaving it to the philosophy of music to explain music's momentousness in terms of its effects upon the emotions. I intend to demonstrate, as in the previous chapter with regard to black popular music, the limitations of stopping with "field 2" analysis (philosophy of music) when we should be engaging in "field 3" archaeology (theomusicology).

As I indicated in the last two chapters, my intention is not to claim that there is nothing of value to be learned from the thinking that philosophers do about music. Indeed, a musicologist could even come to some understanding of Still's music in terms of the traditional philosophical discourse about musical discoverism and musical creationism, a discourse that is especially helpful in distinguishing between the twelve-tone composition of Austrian composers Josef Matthias Hauer and Arnold Schoenberg, a compositional technique they both discovered somewhere between 1919 and 1923. Schoenberg viewed himself to be a composer in the traditional sense of the creative artist who is engaged in personal expression through music, while Hauer rejected the paradigm and viewed himself as but an interpreter of the twelve tones so that listeners could glean an aspect of the eternal law of music.[14] It could be argued that Still leaned toward Hauer's musical metaphysics, toward discoverism, when he said that musical ideas are not entirely new but have appeared in the past in one form or another, that his music did not exist in his own mind as "my music," and that the language of musical ownership is only for the purpose of identification. "Every creator is an instrument through which a message is expressed," Still elaborated. "His technical knowledge exists solely to make that expression intelligible to others. Then, when the creation is complete, it goes out to the world and belongs no longer to the creator, but to those who hear it and for whom it was intended."[15] These ideas lean toward musical discoverism, to be sure, but Still also espoused a creationist philosophy when he said these old-new ideas could be handled in fresh and different ways.[16]

To resolve the question of whether Still was philosophically a discoverist or creationist, however, is to resolve very little, for philosophical questions are but penultimate or mediated questions that, as I argued in the last chapter, only presuppose ultimate questions. An unmediated spiritual archaeology could, among other possibilities, reveal the foundation of and religion inherent to Still's adherence to the meta-style of black art—African rhythm. But I have already addressed this general idea in chapter 1. What I wish to show at present is that a spiritual archaeology that bypasses the mediation of philosophy would also show us that underlying Still's philosophical ideas about music is really a theology he worked out over almost four decades through dialogue with the spirit world.

Still was raised in the church by his mother and grandmother, but by 1936, having moved to Los Angeles two years earlier, he had entered into a new religious orbit that influenced his theology. This is evidenced in an essay of 1936 titled "The Art of Musical Creation," which was published in a theosophical journal. In the essay Still said in explanation of his compositional procedure that he procured his musical motifs through inspiration and then catalogued them in a notebook for later compositional use. If at a given time his notebook had no suitable material, he said, then he would have to "search for it in the invisible world."[17]

By the time Still married in 1939, he and his Jewish

wife, Verna Arvey, had been frequenting spiritualist churches for several years and participating in psychic readings and séances. At this point in Still's creative life it was not unusual for him to speak of having composed on the "astral level" while asleep and for him to believe that the ideas he conceived thereupon found their way into his music. But the most interesting phase in the development of Still's theology of music began in the mid-1950s, when he and his wife had come to believe in the existence of a vast band of spirits which had never been incarnate but were working diligently to help usher to earth the promised Aquarian Age. These "disincarnate beings" were neither the souls of deceased people nor angels, nor those highly developed beings of the flying saucers whom the Stills and many others believed earth people occasionally encountered.[18] Rather, they were "psychic forces" or "light forces" which intermingled among both deceased individuals and human beings on earth. Though these beings had never been incarnate, they were believed to have had the capacity to inhabit human bodies in order to handle whatever emergencies on earth could not be handled by the transference of thought or inspiration to the living.[19]

The Stills believed that the light forces generally worked in and through individuals who were determined to tread the path of love. One such person whom the light forces contacted to transfer their thoughts to the needful world was Marjorie Lange, the wife of Hollywood arranger, composer, and conductor Arthur Lange. Marjorie, as she was known to the "disincarnate beings," was the medium through which the Stills received their spiritual correspondence and entered this new phase of religious involvement and theological thought about music. Sometime during the early- to mid-1930s Marjorie met a woman named Marguerite Place, who was involved with the Ouija Board. Marjorie sat in on some of Marguerite's Ouija sessions and at one point the board announced that she would have her own advisor, which led her to procure her own board.[20] Following her experiments with the Ouija Board, Marjorie moved on to psychic mediumship via automatic writing.[21] The automatic writing coming from the spirit world always began with the salutation "I, Walter," but during the late 1930s the writing started to commence with "we"; and one of Walter's friends among the light forces made humorous reference to the others on their astral plain as "whatchamaycallems."[22] It was during the automatic writing phase of Marjorie's spiritual mediumship that the Stills became involved in an ongoing dialogue with the spirit world, with the "we," the "whatchamaycallems"—the "WWs," as Marjorie nicknamed them.

After a number of instances when the automatic writing commenced with "we," Marjorie inquired as to who the "we" were. The answer was that they were a group of psychic forces whose task was to persuade human beings to think of love as not merely a sentiment but as a force that could assist the beings in the spirit world in delivering the "brotherhood of man" to earth. Through Marjorie, who was to make this knowledge known to key people such as the Stills, Americans were eventually to learn about the spiritual assistance available to them who work for better human relations and who would lead others to this field of endeavor.[23] One of the earliest and perhaps most captivating messages that Still received from the WWs through Marjorie was that if he could express his religious concepts in musical form he would be able to awaken uncountable people to the spiritual power that music has.[24]

This message seems to be the basis of the twenty-minute speech Still prepared to be delivered in September of 1964 at a meeting of the Missionary Society of St. Paul Lutheran Church in Los Angeles. The speech was titled "The Seven Wonders: The Wonder of Music," and Still's aim was to awaken his audience to the fact that music was one of the "seven wonders." To argue this was an easy task for him, he said, because music functioned in his life as more than a wonder, but as a way of life—his work, recreation, and "spiritual consciousness."[25] Music functioned in his life as "spiritual consciousness," he said, because it is very often the channel through which God speaks to human beings.[26] When music such as the blues serves in this divine capacity, Still continued, it is of religious value, but this does not necessarily mean that it has explicit religious usage like church music does in Christian worship: "If it is worthwhile music which appeals to us emotionally and meaningfully, it serves a spiritual purpose, whether it is found in church or not."[27]

Because Still believed music generally speaks for itself better than any verbal descriptions of it, he said to his audience that he would at that point in his lecture move on to the phase of playing excerpts from his compositions. One of the excerpts he played was "Levee Land," one of the series of suites comprising his larger work titled *The American Scene*. In his introduction to this musical example, he said something about his classical music that the likes of Charlotte Mason and Olin Downes did not understand, due to their view of religion and culture as separate in all of western art. Still said, "Most of us will agree that people on all levels of human existence have their own spiritual experiences, and that these may not necessarily parallel each other, nor co-incide with our own. For instance, the Blues have often been considered immoral, yet I have found a great deal of beauty in them. They express the yearning of an oppressed people who hope for a better way of life. This is the feeling I tried to convey in the following excerpt, an original piece in the Blues idiom."[28] Following another excerpt from his opera titled *Highway 1, U.S.A.*, Still concluded his lecture by saying that he hoped he had convinced his audience that as one of the seven wonders, music, which is truly food for the soul, is a human requisite.[29]

In the years to come the WWs explained further to Still that music could serve God as a healing force.[30] But in order for music to be used for such therapeutic purposes, human beings first had to raise the level of their "feeling quality" to at least the level of acuity that the modern human intellect had attained,[31] this being the same reaction against the European Enlightenment philosophy of the intellect dominating the intuitive that we see in Mason, Barnes, and Downes. Still understood instinctively the importance the WWs were placing on raising human beings' "feeling quality," for he was raised hearing his grandmother sing the spirituals. He also played the blues with W. C. Handy's band, performed with Eubie Blake's orchestra for the *Shuffle Along* musical, and arranged jazz scores for Don Voorhees, Sophie Tucker, Artie Shaw, Willard Robison, and Paul Whiteman. To Still the means of raising human beings' "feeling quality" so that music could serve as a healing force was to depend as much on inspiration in composing as on the intellect.

In 1961, Still prepared a speech to be given at South Carolina State College, a black institution in Orangeburg, during which he commented on the importance of inspiration in composing. Answering his own question regarding what inspiration is, he stated, "It comes as a result of lifting the individual to the place where he can contact and assimilate a divine emanation. The layman doesn't realize the extent of the effort required to accomplish this, and yet without that divine spark, our human creative efforts are meaningless. No amount of craftsmanship can compensate for its lack." Three years later, in May of 1964, Still gave an interview for the "Music for Young Listeners" program, aired on KPFK Radio in Los Angeles, and the interviewer asked him to explain the well-published fact that he ended his compositions with the words "With humble thanks to God, the Source of Inspiration." Still responded, "I have done that because I feel that there has been help from other sources without in the creation of musical composition, and I think it only right that that help be acknowledged."[32] This is generally how we should understand his *Psalm for the Living* (1954) for chorus and orchestra. Arvey's text conveys the idea that God is intricately involved with human beings, guiding and inspiring their lives and achievements.

Because Still believed strongly that music should be aesthetically satisfying for the general public in order to help people raise the level of their "feeling quality," he held that musical dissonance should be used sparingly, for specific purposes, and should be balanced with consonance.[33] "Machines surpass man in making ugly sounds: let's leave it to them," Still pleaded, "and return to writing real music."[34] Still's most potent assail against unchecked dissonance was, not surprisingly, replete with ultimate concern, for his ongoing dialogue with the spirit world generally underlayed his musical ideas. He said that he thought it would be wise for listeners to shun dissonant "so-called music" because it is a "destructive force" that can be harmful to those who do not protect themselves against it.[35] If Still was alluding to the time the "disjointed" sounds of Leonard Bernstein's Second Symphony made him feel physically ill,[36] he was now certainly interpreting that occasion theologically.

Arvey's retrospective interpretation of that occasion was also replete with theological references. Her reading of her husband's comment about music being a potentially "destructive force" was that there existed a "sinister force" that promotes such dissonant, ultramodern music.[37] To this she attempted to adjoin some philosophical weight, saying, "Plato's *Republic* warns us that the introduction of a new kind of music must be shunned as imperiling a whole state, for styles of music are never disturbed without effecting the most important political institutions."[38] So, it is this religious concern that was behind Still taking every opportunity to share his musical ideals with composers who could fashion a future American music and that was behind his passionately exhorting composers to return to writing "with heart instead of brains, with love instead of disdain, and with attention to spiritual as well as scientific values."[39] In looking back to Still's lecture on "The Seven Wonders: The Wonder of Music," then, we see that Still perceived the blues to be a model of a heartfelt music, a music of love and healing, and that its secularity was of no consequence in this regard.

All of the exhortation Still received from the WWs around the idea of him embodying his religious concepts in musical form with a predominance of consonant sounds, all in order to awaken people to music's healing power, was intended to help the spiritual forces of love initiate the promised "new era."[40] In the meantime, human beings were to develop qualities of the soul that would enable them to make the transition into this era, an era that would be characterized by a peace and prosperity that the world had never before known.[41] That this eschatology became Still's eschatology is reflected in the last two paragraphs of the final chapter of an autobiography he never completed:

> Men of all races in our country must join forces to bring into being a new era, when brotherly love will triumph. Guiding the destiny of the Americas is a Great Intelligence who has brought to these shores many different groups of people in order that they may merge to form one new race, greater than any single race has ever been before. Those who oppose this, by petty prejudices or huge commercial schemes, are fighting a divine power and in the end will be crushed. Of course, their stubborn persistence may bring suffering to all of us. We may be approaching a period more difficult than any we have had. Those who are prepared, mentally and spiritually, will weather the storm and emerge richer in soul than before.

The next, final paragraph in the unfinished autobiography begins and ends: "We cannot ignore or change our destiny."[42]

This eschatology of the WWs was actually Christological, which reveals its point of tangency with the Christian tradition in which Still was raised. Still believed, as the WWs taught, that Christ would help people who believe in him to prepare mentally and spiritually to "weather the storm" that would precede the promised brighter day. Christ's appearances to various individuals in visions, an indication that he was very close to his earthly flock, was to bring about a revival of thought regarding his teachings. This was important because there was a need for a renewal of an intuitive understanding of what the Christ consciousness really is.[43] "We will say that the new Christ is even now preparing to make his appearance in the earth plane," said the WWs. "This is not a matter of days, months, or even years. It is a happening which comes from the timeless realm, and will be recognized when the time comes in your way of contemplating time."[44] Though Jesus was the first man to receive Christhood and he would "come again," the WWs taught that there would be many in the new era who would attain this consciousness.[45] Still understood himself to be one such person, since he had been spiraling upward through a series of incarnations toward Christhood. Among his earlier incarnations, according to psychic Eva May Carrell, Still had been a musician who solaced the biblical David when depressed, and later had been the biblical St. John, the beloved disciple of Jesus.[46]

Although there is a Christology involved in this "new age" religion, the WWs taught that established religions should no longer claim to have the one and only truth and that people must learn to show respect for different religions.[47] Orthodox religions have their place in the scheme of spiritual progress, the WWs taught, but they surpass their usefulness and become harmful when their doctrines prevent individuals from moving on to higher spiritual phases. "The ones who clutch to their breasts a certain dogmatic religion," the WWs explained, "are in need of that religion and are afraid of opening their arms. They are the arresters of time and the stoppers of progress and the inquisitors of those who dare to do differently than they."[48] Ultimately and ideally, say the WWs, individuals need to establish their own relationship with their deity, so that it would be unnecessary to lean on and glean the approval of organized religion.[49]

All the believers of this "new age" Christian community who had established their own relationship with their deity would dwell on a new continent, a paradisical continent, a land of dreams, which would rise up in the midst of the Pacific Ocean.[50] When asked if this dreamland would be the return of Atlantis, the WWs answered that they did not believe there could be a return of those same conditions but that perhaps there could be a development that rivaled that ancient city.[51] The idea of it all must have fascinated Still, as had the legend of the lost continent of Mu, which was said to have been engulfed in the Pacific Ocean thousands of years ago. Still's composition of 1948 for chamber orchestra and chorus, *The Lost Continent,* was an attempt to capture the character of the music he imagined to have existed on that legendary land.

While *The Lost Continent,* written before Still's interaction with the WWs, shows Still to have been fascinated with legendary history, the composition that best reflects the eschatology he acquired from the WWs is *The Peaceful Land* (1960). That this composition won the award given by the National Federation of Music Clubs in 1961 for an orchestral work dedicated to the United Nations, was to Still a prophecy being fulfilled, for the WWs had been telling him since 1956 that his music would find a natural place in the new era and that this era would find him to be highly successful as a composer.[52] Present in Miami for the premiere of his composition by the University of Miami Symphony Orchestra on October 22 and 23, 1961, Still had prepared a speech to be given at the gala where he would receive his award of $1,500 and hear his composition performed. It was an opportunity for him to convey the eschatological message long taught him by the WWs. He said, "I hope sincerely that *The Peaceful Land* will, in some way, help bring nearer that day when men *will* live together in peace and freedom; when men will at last discover that strife and hatred do not solve problems but, instead, create greater problems; when everyone will realize that our world would be drab indeed if there were no differences between races and nationalities and will strive to let those differences add beauty and variety to the fabric as a whole, rather than a barrier separating one group from another."[53]

It is not simply because of his personal musical taste, then, that Still promoted a music of the heart, a music of love, which gives primary attention to spiritual values. He believed religion and culture (art) should reflect the same societal ideal of harmoniousness—that music should be consonant as religion teaches us life ideally should be—and he demonstrated this viewpoint with reference to the composition he wrote for the Cleveland Symphony Orchestra in 1944: "My *Poem for Orchestra* . . . is based on the theme of the world's desolation after war, the energetic building of a new world, and man's spiritual awakening in drawing closer to God. In keeping with the subject, the opening is purposely dissonant, to express desolation and spiritual poverty. But the thematic material grows more consonant and more melodic as it rises to express man's rapture in approaching God."[54] Still believed that music ought not get caught in the mire of world dissonance by proceeding no further than to reflect that turmoil. Rather, music ought to be, like his *Poem for Orchestra,* prophetic, a model of the ideal society even before human harmony and world peace are actually achieved.

No philosophy of music can lead us to these insights requisite for an understanding of Still's music. Only a spiritual archaeology can provide the appropriate hermeneutical lens through which we can see what Charlotte

Mason and Olin Downes were unable to see about Still: that the archetype of all Still's published articles was "The Art of Musical Creation" (1936), that the greatest of his lectures was "The Seven Wonders: The Wonder of Music" (1964), that the preeminent of all his compositions was *The Peaceful Land* (1960), and that the most telling prophecy about him was that he was once the biblical St. John. It is important to note that behind each of these important ingredients of Still's understanding of his music are ethical implications, implications that the researcher of black music must take seriously as a model for ethics and ethical praxis if a truly "integrative inquiry" is to occur. Theology cannot be ignored and neither can the ethics we will always find when we engage in spiritual archaeology.

Thus it is that I have been going forward in my argument but pushing in the circularity of a ring-shout back toward my prologue. Here comes the final shuffling of my feet to complete that return, during which I will argue for and exemplify a musicological ethics for a fully integrative re-search of black music.

CHAPTER 6

AN ETHICS

In the foregoing chapters I have argued that engaging in a spiritual archaeology with the tools of theomusicology in a re-search of black folk, popular, and classical music leads us eventually to the excavation of an ethics that is as indigenous to black culture as "preaching the blues"—Charlie Spand's kind of preaching: "Just as sure as the good Lord sits in the heaven above, now your life ain't all pleasure unless you be with that one you love." Re-searchers should be led to this point of trying to extract an ethics if for no other reason than the fact that a spiritual archaeology of music leads to a recognition that we are estranged from our selves. This estrangement has occurred by virtue of our maintaining a doctrine of belief that sides the sacred, spiritual, and religious in respective opposition to the profane, sexual, and culture. The recognition of this estrangement should propel us toward reconciliation, for it is the natural impulse of the ethical agent to resolve life's tensions in pursuit of human happiness.

When this realization of our estrangement from our natural selves comes to the theomusicologist, who in response to the reflex toward reconciliation creates a strategy for unknotting the tension, what results is the kind of ethics and praxis that N. Lynne Westfield and Harold Dean Trulear exemplify. From their positions as Christian theomusicologists, they write:

The church's longstanding suspicion of secular music reflects its sense of competing worldviews between church and world, with the result that not much attention has been paid to how "secular" music shapes the theo-ethical perspectives of church youths, save for the standard forays against sex, violence, and drugs.

Theomusicology, for us, becomes a discipline that encourages the investigation of the process of socialization as a fundamentally religious or theological one, whether the data in question is secular music or traditional church music. . . .

This insight, one hopes, would lead to more faithful church programming, especially in Christian education. Those involved in this ministry are working with young people in the business of world-building and the development of value and meaning. Therefore, we must raise questions of meaning at every turn, seeking to assess both the impact of extraparochial influences on young people and to develop clarity about the church's meaning system itself. Teaching—the transmission of meaningful tradition—is therefore a powerful tool in the church's possession.[1]

With this, Westfield and Trulear conclude that they believe teaching to be a vehicle for individual and societal transformation, and that as leaders in the black church they have the responsibility to initiate and participate in this transformation. They say, "theomusicology can help us in this endeavor."[2]

One of the realizations to arise out of Westfield's and Trulear's theomusicological analysis of Hammer is the need of the black church for a sexual ethic. "We have yet to formulate a sexual ethic for ourselves," they say. "We fear our bodies. We either speak too harshly or remain violently silent."[3] But the blues, as I first suggested in my prologue, is neither silent nor harsh when it comes to the topic of sex. Beneath all of the lyric about a man's "snake" and a woman's "jellyroll" and about lovers doing the "bedspring pop," there is a seedling of a sexual ethic to be extracted if musicologists would be willing to engage in the requisite spiritual archaeology. That ethic, when articulated, includes the kind of preaching that Bessie Smith did in her "Preachin' the Blues" of 1927. Smith confessed to the "girls" that her intention in singing her song was not to save their souls but rather to advise them practically as to how to preserve their "jellyrolls." She continued with her blues biblicism, "Read on down to chapter 10, taking other women's men you are doin' a sin." Big Bill Broonzy, in his "Preaching the Blues," similarly called out those women who go to church just to show their skirts and those men who go just to hide their dirt. He specifically warned the "brother" who occasionally had his way with married women that he had better get on his knees and pray both night and day because he could end up going to hell that way. There is a day coming, Broonzy prophesied, when Gabriel will blow his trumpet and judgment will come. "Brother what you gonna do," he asked?

Blues singers spoke so openly because their prophetic "calling" was, as Reverend Rubin Lacy reminds us, to sing the truth. Lacy said to his congregation one day that he used to be a famous blues singer and told more truth in his blues than the average churchgoer tells in church songs.[4] Thus, if we are going to flush out completely Samuel Floyd's petition for an integrative inquiry into black music, inquiry that moreover is substantially indigenously derived, particularly derived from black folk music,[5] then we must not overlook the results of what our spiritual archaeology of black music uncovers for us—a potential ethics.

A thorough review of the literature of the historical, philosophical, and social science musicologies reveals hardly any effort to carry out this kind of pursuit, almost certainly because the analytical paradigms for scholarship in these other disciplines are based on a presumed division between the sacred and the profane. Simply put, how could the British scholar Paul Oliver come anywhere close to finding an ethics in the blues when his Victorian partitioning of life's unity causes him to conclude that the blues are "somewhat bereft of spiritual values?"[6] Oliver proves Floyd correct, that a more "culture-derived" approach is needed because there are many aspects of black music that European-derived analysis will not uncover.[7] Theomusicology, already indigenously derived as I explained in chapter 2, possesses the tools of spiritual archaeology and has begun to excavate an ethics and ethical praxis indigenous to black culture.

Despite this phenomenal find, there has been no rush for the gold. Indeed, the response of scholars in the established musicologies, such as historical musicologist David Burrows, is that academic entities should not be multiplied without dire need. Burrows concludes that, in his judgment, theomusicology fails the test of necessity because its concerns are "regularly" accommodated within historical musicology and ethnomusicology.[8] This is a view probably held by most orthodox musicologists, who, paradoxically, probably would also agree with how narrowly Burrows actually defines the traditional disciplines as "regularly" accommodated. "Philosophy," defines Burrows, "typically represents music as being 'all of music,' and devotes little close analysis to particular performances. Ethnomusicology takes music to be inseparable from its contexts and may deal with representations of both performance and context in fine detail. A musicologist specialized in European music of privilege might devote a chapter to a history of style over the course of a century, or give the same amount of attention to one contredanse."[9]

I alluded in chapter 2 that ethnomusicologists who pursue the self-reflexive fieldwork account could reveal how music puts people in touch with that which is common to all human beings. They could consequently remind us of an ethic—the common human make-up of people across societies. But ethnomusicologists never posit an ethical let alone practical use for the data they uncover.

Generally they seem satisfied with their defined roles and happily go about contributing to the history and study of music by remedying the lack of documentation on "non-literate" or "illiterate" societies.

For instance, when ethnomusicologists seek to demonstrate explicitly that the music of subordinated female subcultures in non-western societies is as musically authentic and culturally significant as male-dominated western music, it is difficult to determine whether they are arguing vicariously for the liberation of the subordinated or, amid a spectrum of possibilities, simply for their own legitimate place in the intellectual discourse of musicology. Ethics cannot be left to be guessed at, yet the uncertainty of intention is exactly what we get, for instance, in Ellen Koskoff's edited book, *Women and Music in Cross-Cultural Perspective* (1989). The book addresses the effect of inter-gender relations and gender-related behaviors on music performance and culture, which gives rise to two central questions that Koskoff says each of the articles in the book addresses: first, the degree to which a society's ideologically motivated gender-related behaviors have an impact on musical thought and practice; and second, the way in which a society's music functions to reflect and affect inter-gender relations.[10]

JaFran Jones's article, "A Sociohistorical Perspective on Tunisian Women as Professional Musicians," is the ideal piece with which to raise the question of what drives the ethnomusicologist to traverse other worlds. I have chosen Jones because she was one of the two ethnomusicologists at the theomusicology forum that, as I reported in chapter 2, I held at Bowling Green State University in 1991. Her comments at the forum demonstrated the hesitancy of ethnomusicologists to engage in a broad-sweeping spiritual archaeology of the cultures they study, while her article in Koskoff's book reveals the hesitancy of ethnomusicologists to make practical ethical use of the knowledge they uncover. At the theomusicology forum, Jones admitted that ethnomusicologists, in trying to come to grips with the momentousness of music, prefer to talk about aesthetics because they feel uncomfortable with the idea of spirituality. In her article in Koskoff's book, she demonstrates that ethnomusicologists also consider it beyond their domain to engage in ethics.

In her article Jones makes a comment that in fact characterizes all of the ethnomusicological pieces in Koskoff's book. She says her aim is to give an historical voice to the long-silenced women's musical culture in the Islamic society of Tunisia and that it will be left up to "other specialists" to address the "broader" social, legal, and *ethical* dimensions.[11] In a rather objective way, typical of the ethnomusicologist as social scientist, Jones shows that Tunisian women have increasingly improved their social status, as reflected in the musical culture of their society, and she only slips in a muted warning at her article's close—that a resurgence of religious fundamentalism throughout the Islamic world threatens the advancements Tunisian women have made.[12] Jones's muted warning is part and parcel of her leaving the broader social, legal, and ethical dimensions of the implications of her scholarship to other specialists. I contend that this results from the same male-domination that typifies the origin and character of one of ethnomusicology's parent disciplines, anthropology.

In contrast, the unique piece in Koskoff's book is by Carol Robertson, the Argentinean ethnomusicologist whom I mentioned in chapter 2 as one of the six discussants on the "Ethnics and Ethnomusicology" panel at the 1991 meeting of the Society for Ethnomusicology. Robertson was the panelist who was especially direct about ethnomusicology's devaluation of ideas regarding music's relationship to spirituality, about the avoidance of "sentimentality" in ethnomusicological scholarship, and about the need for self-reflexivity and storytelling in ethnomusicology. Her article in Koskoff's book, "Power and Gender in the Musical Experiences of Women," is no doubt placed at the end because it exemplifies Robertson's desire to transgress the traditional boundaries of ethnomusicology and even to engage in ethical thinking.

In her cross-cultural study of six musical cultures in northern Ghana, Andean Argentina, South America, and North America (including Washington, D.C.), Robertson examines the ways in which music functions as a mediator of power between the genders. She recognizes that the means by which women use music performance as an instrument of power to challenge authority is dependent on societal administrative style and, more specifically, the culture's theological, mythological, and ceremonial sanctions of that style.[13] She discusses the importance of myths and their androcentric subtexts that are "designed" to control women's lives, and she references the biblical myth of the "temptation of Eve" as holding some interesting parallels with the mythologies of several of the societies she studied.[14] Given all of this, when Robertson says the study of music in emerging cultures has "broad implications" for understanding musical, political, and theological change in any culture,[15] she has engaged in the move from historical exegesis to critical hermeneutics (ethics) and pointed the way toward ethical praxis.

Now I will give an example of a theomusicological piece in which the ethical intent of the research is fully unmasked from the outset. In his article titled "On Jazzology," Michael Jarrett confronts the hegemony of "counterfeit" jazz musicology, by which he means amateur musicology that has been allowed to pass for authentic scholarship because it reinforces the high self-image and imperialism of western civilization. "What amateur criticism loved in jazz was not some religious or spiritual essence," says Jarrett, "but in fact its own image; what this culture saw reflected in amateur representation of jazz was not the god of jazz, but ultimately itself."[16] Jarrett shows, as an illustration, that Gunther Schuller's *Early Jazz* (1968) is comprised of counterfeit musicology because it uses western musicology to "colonize" jazz and lend it "legitimacy."[17] He concludes by suggesting that theomusicology find the appropriate language of discourse to avoid counterfeiting and to write authentically on jazz in a way that will not harm its authentic "spirit."[18]

Given Jarrett's challenge to theomusicology, and given my criticisms of the established musicologies, of the three paradigms ethnomusicologist Daniel Neuman identifies regarding the ways in which history is addressed in his discipline, only the "reflexive" and "immanent" modes are of primary interest to theomusicology as regards a musicological ethics. "In the reflexive mode," says Neuman, "the essays are about the history of musicological debates: the community is musicologists and the authors, their descendants. In the interpretive mode, the essays are about modern music history: the community is the 'other,' and the authors are outsiders. In the immanent mode, the essays are about music constructing history: the ethnic group is the 'other,' and the authors are co-authors."[19] *Reflexive music history*, to be more specific, comprises an actual historicizing of music historiography, such that the form and intents of a particular musicological approach to history are the subjects of documentation.[20] *Interpretive music history* consists of, in part, an externally constructed history of a particular musical culture that is intended to contribute to world music history and its study.[21]

Regarding this latter, I contend that the re-searcher of black music should never stop at doing history for the sake of its external documentation. Our re-search suggests that ideally it should proceed to *immanent music history*, where music is a source of the history of its creator's and consumer's community. From there the re-searcher should ideally proceed to what can be termed *salvational music history*—a reading of the "soul history" of individuals and communities for the purpose of engaging our ethics in a praxis informed by the mythological and theological orientations of religious human beings. In other words, once Robertson's "immanent music history" has revealed the androcentric subtexts of societal myths, and her referencing the biblical myth of the "temptation of Eve" as holding parallels with the mythologies of the societies she studied, then we should proceed with our "salvational" criticism of the mythological root at which the problems lie.

For instance, if we were re-searching black hymnody where the problem of sexism if not misogyny abounds, then we must engage in the requisite ethical response. As regards the dilemma surrounding gender and hymnody, hymnologist Helen Pearson suggests that her disciplinary colleagues engage in "hymnic exegesis" in order to ask certain critical questions about the text, just as biblical scholars engage in scriptural exegesis.[22] However, in order to carry out such hymnic exegesis to the necessary degree, so that we get at the very mythological root of these dilemmas, I contend that musicologists must also engage in biblical exegesis. Since scriptural myths and writings have been misused in the past to perpetuate the problems surrounding gender, I contend that gender discrimination is still a symptom of a mythological flaw. I think this mythological flaw is what is repeatedly hinted at when scholars speak of the deeper or subconscious causes of discrimination.

Music scholars of an ethical sensibility, a sensibility that is naturally nurtured by doing spiritual archaeology, can address these deeper or subconscious causes of discrimination against black women by searching out the original meaning of Genesis 3:1–6, a segment of the larger narrative (Genesis 2:4b–3:24) whose setting is the Garden of Eden.[23] The episode of temptation and disobedience involving the characters of Eve, Adam, and the serpent has been used by the early church fathers of the Greco-Roman world and their sons of European civilization to develop and perpetuate the dogmatic tradition of patriarchy—the ideology of male supremacy—and a hymnody that has been the curse of women ever since. Did Eve really beguile an innocent Adam and thus deservingly receive a punishment that has been and will continue to be transmitted to every woman of every generation in the form of gender subordination? Were the early dogmaticians correct in naming this event the "fall"—the origination of "original sin"—and in placing its responsibility on Eve (and every woman)? In a word, who was really to blame for the problem of female subjugation, Eve (and every woman) or the early church fathers and their sons (every man)?

In general, androcentric readings of this myth in Catholicism, Protestantism, and secular popular culture have adversely affected religious doctrines, ethical theories, civil laws, social customs, and personal characterizations. This tradition, perpetuated in church liturgies via the sexist language and images of hymnody, has caused deception and fostered human oppression rather than liberation. To discover the real Eve of the biblical myth, as musicologists of an ethical sensibility ought to try to do, will be to begin to see the damage the guardians of biblical orthodoxy have wreaked on certain constituencies of the so-called "beloved community."

My presupposition is that women's emancipation is not just a private, domestic issue, but is the concern of all societies deeply entrenched in the multiple oppressions of gender, race, and class. This then is a quest for the full emancipation of women and the true equality between the sexes, not for the so-called "equal rights" held by a minority of women belonging to the elite classes, women who are sometimes ultra-conservative and essentially male in their disposition toward women in general. When full emancipation is achieved, when a gender-neutral society is reached, it will be recognizable in statistics that show that gender violence—sexual harassment and assault, domestic violence, and rape—ceases to be the problem that it currently is throughout the world. Musicologists such as JaFran Jones should take it upon themselves to be the "specialists" who show that fallenness has less to do with Eve than it does with a subordinationist orthodoxy that has perpetuated these social problems.

However, this ethical proclamation is the major juncture at which theomusicology, with its spiritual archaeology resulting in an ethical sensibility and praxis, diverges from the historical, philosophical, and the social scientific musicologies as traditionally practiced and defined. What therefore generally sets theomusicology apart from the other musicologies are its explicit concerns for such religious values as human emancipation, including the emancipation of human beings from the estrangement they have with their natural selves. This emancipatory aspect of theomusicology, from a social rather than psychological perspective, can be defined in terms of what African American philosopher Cornel West calls "prophetic pragmatism," an offshoot of the tradition of American pragmatism represented by Ralph Waldo Emerson, William James, and John Dewey. West's intellectual praxis, largely influenced by W. E. B. Du Bois's pragmatic manner, is a product of prophetic Protestant Christianity. It is philosophy as cultural criticism for the purpose of causing social change—increasing individual development, democratic operations, existential sustenance, political relevance, and human progress.[24]

Based on a redefinition of earlier pragmatic traditions, for the sake of including a more explicitly political and praxis-oriented cultural criticism rooted in religion,[25] prophetic pragmatism seeks to reinvigorate critical intelligence and sophisticated scholarship in America and to promote a culture of creative democracy as a means of regenerating social forces that can empower the marginalized.[26] This kind of ethical impetus is what is missing from the traditional musicologies but is requisite for theomusicology. Divinity scholar Clyde Steckel agrees, saying: "I am in full agreement with Spencer's call for the socially transforming character of theomusicology. A theological interpreter of music is never free just to observe and analyze the way in which a culture's music expresses its religious meanings. A theological interpreter is always interpreting and analyzing *for the sake of* that more blessed state of God's restored justice and peace which music can so powerfully express."[27]

The black literary critic Houston Baker also has in mind a prophetic pragmatism, albeit one without the explicit theological language that we find in West and Steckel. Concerned about the devaluation of black literature resulting from the use of non-indigenous measurements, Baker says that if an investigator's efforts are sufficiently "charged with blues energy," the investigator is almost certain to bring a more appropriate perspective to the literary criticism.[28] He continues: "A properly trained critic—one versed in the vernacular and unconstrained by traditional historical determinants—may well be able to discover blues inscriptions and liberating rhythms even in some familiarly neglected works of Afro-American expressive culture. Who, after all, has dismissed such works? Normally, they have been written off by commentators (black and white alike) constrained by a single standard of criticism. Who is to decipher such neglected expressive instances? Surely, the blues critic is the most likely agent."[29]

If we read Baker's notion of the energized blues critic through the hermeneutic of our spiritual archaeology, I think what we would come up with is the blues critic engaging in what Molefi Asante calls the "soul of method." This method, which intervenes in the methodological process in order to bring a certain spiritual character to scholarly inquiry, involves the re-searcher accessing the vitality of a project in order to activate the kind of creative energies (let us called them "blues energies") that seek comprehension for the sake of harmony and that avoid prediction for the sake of control.[30] "One breaks the structured, lineal monotony by investing research with soul," explains Asante, "the rhythm of assessing and synthesizing in order to create understanding and meaning."[31] I think art historian Robert Farris Thompson would say of the "soul of method" and the theomusicologist's quest for it: "This to me is an example of how love, and also religious passion as an aspect of love, far from destroying objectivity, can push us to an objectivity beyond all academic understanding."[32]

The antithesis of this religious passion in scholarship is exemplified by Stanley Hauerwas, a Christian ethicist who admits to writing just for the financial gain it brings. In the preface of one of his books, Hauerwas's very first words are: "Contrary to popular opinion I do not have a compulsion to write. On the contrary, ... I write because people ask me to read a paper about this or that for this or that amount of money and since I always need money I write. I believe that Samuel Johnson was right that anyone who does not write for money is a fool."[33] Hauerwas's reason for writing lacks "soul." The theomusicologist's reasons for writing, conversely, are not financial but genuinely theological. They are what the Christian ethicist's reasons for writing ought to be—wholeness and fulfillment, both of which are symbolized by the ring of the ring-shout and the trickster figure who was a part of the ring ceremony in Africa and America.

Because I have spoken so passionately about these ideals that derive from the spiritual archaeology spawned by theology, one ethnomusicologist accused me of resurrecting medieval arrogance and recrowning theology "queen."[34] Another ethnomusicologist stated similarly that theomusicology makes claims of "philosophical superiority" over the other musicological disciplines.[35] But in the day that theology was perceived to be "queen," never to be omitted from any scholarly inquiry, such men of letters as the early seventeenth century French priest Mersenne (Marinus Mersennus) believed music was to be understood by means of analogy with such concepts of Christian theology as the trinity.[36] The intent of establishing theomusicology as the ideal means for re-searching black music is not to return to such days when music histories were dominated by ecclesiastical authority, biblical periodization, and the "divine origins" theory—the age when music was the "hand-maid of religion." I am not trying to argue that theology is queen but that science, which has ruled in the West since the European Enlightenment, should not be. For one reason, science is unaccepting of the kind of religious passion that would permit musicology to integrate ethics into its inquiry. Thus, I agree with Langdon Gilkey: "To confine knowledge to one method, and to a method that abstracts away from all subjectivity, centeredness and uniqueness, is infinitely to constrict the world that is real to us in its depth and mystery; it is to objectify into a determined, subjectless realm all that with which we have to do."[37] As Gilkey says of science, "The queen can save herself from banishment only if—as religion had to do— she is willing to abdicate her role as queen."[38] In agreement with Gilkey, I proposed in chapter 2 that theology and the social sciences balance one another, that they should balance one another like theory and praxis should. With ethics then being permitted to be a part of the musicological discipline, a true "integrative inquiry" in the re-search of black music would be possible.

I can think of no better balance between science and theology and between theory and praxis than in the work of Nicholas Cooper-Lewter, whom I mentioned in chapter 2 as one of the speakers at the theomusicology forum I held at Bowling Green State University in 1991. It was Cooper-Lewter's license with self-reflexivity that ethnomusicologist Stephen Cornelius complained about as failing to keep the personal, social, and musical experiences separate from one another. Yet it was the integration of personal, social, and musical experiences that led to Cooper-Lewter's discovery of the integration of theology and psychotherapy in a musicological praxis (theomusicotherapy) that he calls "soul therapy."

Cooper-Lewter's "soul therapy," whereby he prescribes music for the healing process of his clients, was a system that had its beginnings in his integrated personal, social, and musical experiences in the 1960s while an undergraduate student at a Christian liberal arts college in Ohio farm country. Cooper-Lewter explained to the audience at the theomusicology forum at Bowling Green that he and the few other black students at the college dealt with the corrosion of their psychological well-being by submerging themselves in the "soul-healing" sounds of black music during midweek "secular prayer meetings." With reference to the Temptations' song "Keep On Rollin' Along," he said:

> Often we could say nothing of what we were really feeling or thinking if we were to remain in college... so we mobilized our collective heritage of "soul" in order to just keep rollin' along. Out of the sustained racial hostility and injustice at our school emerged this shared experience of power and perseverance, and the music of the Temptations was therapy.
>
> In more technical terms, because we were subsisting in a deceptively camouflaged Jim Crow infrastructure that voraciously devoured the reserves in our belief systems, the "ministry" of the Temptations helped us shift out of a "left brain" mode and brought us relief from the linear logic of a supercompetitive existence within a Eurocentric dichotomous reality. We needed and received "grace treatments" in order to remain free of a tempting neurotic dependence on the approval or acceptance of the white majority....
>
> The Temptations ministered to our souls, for we allowed their words to subdue the insults that daily weakened our sense of well-being. In opening the way for all sectors of our consciousness to get recharged (the rational, intuitive, and emotive), we danced and sang our agreement with what the Temp-

tations seemed to understand about our personal and collective deprivations in this hostile white environment. Their lyrics and sounds occasionally permitted us to carve out space where we could take deep breaths, submerge ourselves in soul, and then emerge from within the interstices of our victimization to become co-protectors of one another.[39]

Before continuing with Cooper-Lewter's story of how he came to merge personal, social, and musical experiences into an ethical praxis, I will corroborate his testimony about how black music functioned in a healing way for black youths coming from their own communities into predominantly white ones. William C. Turner, Jr., similarly recalling his years in the early 1960s as part of the first generation of blacks to integrate Duke University, said he and his black colleagues drew sustenance from the music of the Impressions:

> The Impressions—first with lead singer Jerry Butler and later Curtis Mayfield—were characterized by a mellow, sweet, soothing sound. The harmony was so close that it could slide between the creases of sadness and joy. It could drive one into the intensely private places where contact could be made with the most deeply felt emotions. With their crescendos the Impressions made us feel that it was alright to be who you were and to have a good time. Their sounds were powerful, much like those produced in the music of the black church. . . .
> Pushing out into the larger world from the womb of the black community was the mission of the Impressions' generation. With the help of these gentlemen of song, "pushing" took place to the tune of music that had long been the property of black people. "Keep on pushing" was the needed encouragement when suddenly we were among the few of our race in the newly integrated schools. Where once we had been the intellectual stars, we now were banished to the social periphery of the predominantly white schools. . . . Daily explanations were requested for manners, preferences, and values that were so much a part of us that we never noticed them. We were the objects of observation and suspicion. Thus, for those who integrated dormitories, football squads, glee choirs, and fraternities, it did us a world of good to hear melodic strains that said, "Keep on

pushing." Without pushing we would have been bruised and hurt. Pushing came to be an orientation to life, an attitude within the new cosmos, a gesture toward a different sort of history. Pushing was the posture that produced our future.[40]

It was this "pushing" or "rolling" out into the larger world from the womb of the black community that fell upon the Impressions' and Temptations' generation, which, if Cooper-Lewter's and Turner's stories can be generalized, caused that generation to integrate their personal, social, and musical experiences into a healing "soul therapy." But, it was Cooper-Lewter, trained in psychology, and having done some work in divinity as well, who developed this self-nurture of his college days into a professional praxis. He recalled:

> It became increasingly evident to me that the "soul therapy" of black culture was informed and infused by music—sounds and meanings replete with wellsprings of empowerment. The evidence is that no other people in history, so abjectly severed from their natural way of life as were the Africans enslaved in America, had come through slavery having created an immense body of soul-mending songs—the spirituals. It was in thinking about this, in light of the therapeutic use of music by my college friends, that the idea of building a professional music-based "soul therapy" came to me. Clearly, my development of a therapeutic model using theological music that helps heal the whole person was not, as I pursued the healing profession, an option for me; it was my destiny.[41]

What Cooper-Lewter calls "the wellsprings of empowerment" in black music, I explained in chapter 1 as the reintensifying rhythms found in black ritual places. Those ritual places include such spaces as those Cooper-Lewter and his college classmates carved out in "the interstices of our victimization" for their midweek "secular prayer meetings." I also suggested in chapter 1 that we understand this weekly cycle as a swing to and from what I called the trickster's rhythms, a swing that Martin Buber calls the "two primary metacosmical movements of the world,"[42] and Bruce Reed calls "oscillation" between human intradependence and spiritual extradependence.[43] I said in that chapter that in these ritual places, whether sacred places (such as the church) or secular (such as the blues joint), rhythm provides both the pulse and the impulse hand-in-hand; and the experiences of gathering, greeting, singing, testifying, dance, trance, and collapse gives black people the reintensified strength needed to face again the structured and often oppressive workaday world. But in addition to the healing aspect of the "sounds" (the rhythms) of black music, Cooper-Lewter gives credence to the "meanings." We gather this as he goes on to explain the process by which his "soul therapy" actually heals, thus also illustrating the importance of ethical praxis:

> As I developed my understanding of the healing profession, I learned that people bring to any "helping relationship" a system of core beliefs that aid them in their survival and that our "soul music" can inform and support those beliefs. Core beliefs are acquired through life experiences and are planted and cultivated by music. These core beliefs are sacred and must be appreciated as the best psychological anchors people have relied on to balance them amid life's difficult passages. To depreciate the belief system or the musical means by which it is informed and supported, as has been done to African-American music by significant segments of the larger culture, vitiates the nurture and care such forms afford.... To use the term coined in theomusicology, the system of "theomusicotherapy" that emerged from my appreciation of the way "soul" music supports our system of core beliefs has as its object the tapping and development of intuitively experienced and affirmed values derived from the triadic relationship between self, others, and God.
>
> To be able to draw holistically on one's core beliefs, while being fed in the "soul," is the goal of my theomusicotherapy. The strategic emphasis of this therapy hinges on effectively eliciting and/or planting healthy core beliefs in the intuitive and the emotive sectors of consciousness with the help of a pre-

scribed musical diet. Theologically speaking, a pivotal goal of this theomusicotherapeutic approach to healing is to help people experience God as a coherent and dependable Being under whom is operative a wholesome set of values, ethics, and mythologies.[44]

Cooper-Lewter has thus reached the laudable goal that Paul Tillich could only argue for—the broadening of the term theology to include its relationship to psychoanalysis, which relationship is most conspicuous in the counselor who gives counsel concurrently in religious and psychoanalytic terms. My joining Tillich with regard to the laudability of this kind of project has nothing to do with the notion of theology being queen or theomusicology claiming "philosophical superiority" over the other musicological disciplines. Moreover, as for the warning of ethnomusicologist Stephen Cornelius, who argued at the Bowling Green theomusicology forum that we ought to keep the personal, social, and musical experiences separate, and like-minded people who think we should keep psychoanalysis and theology separate, I also agree with Tillich that, "If these common roots are found, the question of the relationship of psychoanalysis and theology is brought into a larger and more fundamental framework. Then it is possible to reject the attempts of some theologians and some psychologists to divide these two realms carefully and give to each of them a special sphere. It is then possible to disregard those people who tell us to stay in this or that field: here a system of theological doctrines and there congeries of psychological insights. This is not so. The relationship is not one of existing alongside each other; it is a relationship of mutual interpenetration."[45]

In the light of Cooper-Lewter's work in meshing theology and psychoanalysis, my prologue was but a layperson's attempt to be a counselor and healer for the Greenwood congregation I spoke to during the Mississippi Delta's Blues Week. I was engaging in a prophetic pragmatism derived from my occupation as a theomusicologist. But my positing of an ethics to the church, an ethics I believe to be indigenous to black culture, was done in an arena that at its best naturally provides a "soul therapy." To oscillate regularly or normatively to and from the extradependence of the black church is ideally to participate in a caretaking experience, for there is singing, and the songs encourage and counsel worshippers; there is preaching, and the best preaching is that which is imbued with the understanding of pastoral care and counseling; and there is storytelling, and those who are narrative theologians speak of the importance of telling stories and sharing them with the community, for what one person has come through in their own personal experiences others can then know they too can "come through." The latter, known as testifying, involves a merging of personal, social, and musical experiences. The use of the language of a hymn as the primary language in the testifying that follows the singing of that hymn suggests what Cooper-Lewter said about the intent of "soul therapy" to elicit or plant healthy core beliefs in the intuitive and the emotive parts of the consciousness with the assistance of a prescribed musical diet. What we see, then, is that Cooper-Lewter's "soul therapy" has roots in both the sacred (the church) and secular (the blues joint) ritual places of black people where the sounds (rhythms) and meanings of black music merge with and become religion.

The point is (and this is another ethical implication of my prologue) that perhaps the most healthy individuals are the ones who go both to the Saturday night function and the Sunday morning function, those who can sing songs of gladness when they are "in heaven" and songs of sadness when they are "in hell." This is more or less what I said to the two theological faculty whom I met and talked to at length at the University of Fort Hare in South Africa during the summer of 1992. Shortly after my return to the United States, I received a letter from one of the university's music faculty, Jonah Van Dyk, to whom the information about theomusicology had been passed. The music professor concluded his letter by writing of theomusicology, "I believe that the Music Department at the University of Fort Hare is ripe for the implementation of such a course in our curriculum, and I see your visit here as a part of a Godly plan to make disciples of all nations."

There is a season for all things, and this seems to be the season in which musicologists interested in black music are being summoned to begin re-searching it with an "integrative inquiry," an inquiry that I have argued should be spearheaded by a spiritual archaeology that will unearth, among other knowledges, all kinds of potentialities for an ethics indigenous to black culture.

CONCLUSION

There is an old southern tale about a white man, a Jewish man, and a black man, whose differences were the subject of God's curiosity. God wanted to see whether each of these men would take advantage of the opportunity to get into heaven with but a dollar's toll. The white man was given his dollar and went straight to the heavenly gates, where he paid to get in. The Jewish man went up to the gates and claimed only to have ninety-nine cents, but was also let in. The black man, as Lee Drake tells the tale, made a few stops before heading heavenward: "Well, this Negro, he had done stopped and brought him a brand new suit. He got dead sharp, cool; as sharp as a tack, cool as a cucumber. He had a quarter left. He stopped by the liquor house and got him a quarter-shot of liquor. Got about high. And so later on, 'bout the shank of the evening, this Negro staggered up and knocked on the door: bop, bop, bop, bop! Say, 'Whatcha say there J.C.?' Say, 'How much is it to go to heaven?' My Lord told him, say, 'One dollar.' He [the man] say, 'Well, can I pay you Saturday?' He [the Lord] say, 'Naw, go on back down yonder to hell.' So he messed up; he had to go to hell!"[1]

The stereotypes that favor the white man and Jewish man in this story being told by a black man need not perplex us if we presume that such tales are on the one hand cathartic fun-making, and on the other hand elaborations on kernels of core belief. As folklorist James Aswell says of the storyteller with respect to the latter, "Because his words will not be weighed, judged, and held against his morals or character, his stories are most apt to reveal what he really thinks about life and death, religion, and his fellow men than does his public attitude toward these things."[2]

If we look past the fun-making, then, we must consider the possibility that the black man in the tale did not want to go to heaven, a possibility that should be considered in light of the fact that it was a Judeo-Christian heaven (as symbolized by the Jewish and white men who wanted to go there and were admitted). By pursuing the idea that the black man did not want to go to heaven, we will not only find that this disinterest has wide precedence in the secular black community but that it also has roots that lay in the African cosmology that came to the New World during the European slave trade. Perhaps the reason blues singers often seemed so disrespectful of heaven, indicating that the only heaven in which they would want to dwell would be a heaven of their own, is because the African cosmology that survived the diaspora did not include the concept of people going to heaven. The Creator lived in "heaven," but the spirit of a living person did not descend from heaven and the living spirit of a deceased person did not return there.[3] This cosmology may very well explain what Son House meant in his blues titled "My Black Mama": "Yeah it ain't no heaven now and it ain't no burning hell; said I, where I'm going when I die can't nobody tell."

Furthermore, secular blacks who were unaccepting of the Judeo-Christian cosmology tended to find the God of the Judeo-Christian heaven to be too tolerant of negative aspects of human nature, such as the racism that pushed J. T. "Funny Papa" Smith to complain in "Howling Wolf Blues" that it seemed that God did not treat him like he was humankind. From the perspective of blues people like Funny Papa, this was the same God who permitted the white man and Jewish man, about whom Lee Drake storied, into heaven despite their flaws—the white man being the principal cause of black people singing the blues and the Jewish man presenting only ninety-nine cents to pay the required toll of one dollar to get in heaven.

Moreover, this God who was too tolerant of negative aspects of human nature was also too intolerant of the positive aspects of human nature, such as a man's natural love for his woman or a woman's natural love for her man. This God was not only unaccepting of the blues, which he considered "devil's music," but was also unaccepting of Charlie Spand's quite righteous belief: "Just as sure as the good Lord sits in the heaven above, now your life ain't all pleasure unless you be with that one you love." So, God's heavenly music would be that religiously ingenuine music of the church, such as "When I Take My Vacation in Heaven," music that Reverend Rubin Lacy said neglected to tell the truth. Why then would the black man in the tale Drake tells want to go to that God's heaven if that God would not permit black people to sing the truth about how the rentman evicted him, how the bossman cheated him, how the lawman wrongly convicted him, and how his woman left him? What was this black man to do but gladly accommodate J. C.: "Naw, go on back down yonder to hell." At least "in hell" the black man could still sing the blues and amidst that seeming profaneness call on the name of the Lord: "oh Lord," "good Lord," "Lordy Lordy," "Lord have mercy," "the good Lord above," "my God," "God knows," "for God's sake," "I declare to God," "so help me God," "great God almighty!" For the Psalm says, "if I make my bed in hell, behold, thou art there."

But what about the return "home," the completed journey which I said in my prologue makes the "prodigal son" story so extraordinarily profound to the religious imagination? What about the sacred circularity of the ring-shout, which I said represents unendingness, wholeness, fulfillment? If the black man in the tale Drake tells has squandered his dollar on clothes and liquor, then the next stages in the narrative logically must have him falling into utter destitution, then realizing how better off he was before leaving "home," and finally returning to the place whence he had come. Indeed, the narrative of circularity still holds true if the ring-shout is selected as not just the symbol of circularity but of cosmology, a selection I have alluded to since my prologue when I compared the return of the prodigal son specifically to the circularity of the ring-shout. Too, in chapter 1, when I quoted Sterling Stuckey about the likely close connection between the ring and the African trickster, I implied that the ring-shout and the trickster symbolize the same wholeness.[4]

The ring-shout, then, represents an alternative cosmology to the Judeo-Christian tradition—a different point of beginning and ending in the circular process of going and returning. In this cosmology human existence does not have its beginning or ending with the Creator in heaven. Rather, a person begins as this-worldly spirit and returns to the world of the spirits for continued life after death. The vicinity of earth has always been the "home" of African peoples and their ancestors in the African cosmology perpetuated clandestinely in the ring-shout, the thematizing and personifying of the trickster, and in the spirituals, blues, jazz, rhythm and blues, soul, pop, and rap.

We have always presumed that the spirituality of black secular music was gleaned from an overflow of the spirituality generated and perpetuated in the black church, and I myself contributed to that belief in chapter 4. The notion of black church spirituality overflowing into secular music is not incorrect, but there is a reciprocal flow—that flow into the church from the outside. I am speaking of the currents carried by those prodigal sons and daughters who had been off in a "foreign land," who returned to the church to preach or sing.

Thus, the institution of the black church and the culture the black church spawned drew significantly from the institution of black (secular) music. The canonical authority of this latter institution that has been unincorporated and unrecognized is that of the black trickster, the theology of the crossroads, the cosmology of the ringshout. From this collective source of normativity, an alternative to the sources of normativity maintained by the black church, we can derive an indigenous black ethics. To re-search black music with a holistic "integrative studies" is to discover this and to pursue it.

NOTES

FOREWORD

1. For the original version see Jon Michael Spencer, "If I Make My Bed in Hell," *Black Sacred Music: A Journal of Theomusicology* 8, no. 2 (Fall 1994): 94–98.
2. Cited in Paul Oliver, *Conversation with the Blues* (New York: Horizon, 1965), 169–70.
3. Ibid., 168.
4. Ibid., 160, 168.

INTRODUCTION

1. Samuel A. Floyd, Jr., "On Integrative Inquiry: Toward a Common Scholarship," *CBMR* [Center for Black Music Research] *Digest* 6, no. 1 (Winter 1993): 1.
2. Ibid.
3. Ibid.
4. Ibid.
5. Ibid., 2.
6. Jon Michael Spencer, *Theological Music: Introduction to Theomusicology* (Westport, Conn.: Greenwood, 1991), xii.
7. Clyde J. Steckel, "How Can Music Have Theological Significance?" in *Theomusicology*, ed. Jon Michael Spencer, special issue of *Black Sacred Music: A Journal of Theomusicology* 8, no. 1 (Spring 1994): 20.
8. Floyd, "On Integrative Inquiry," 3.
9. Spencer, *Theological Music,* 96.
10. Edgar W. Schneider, *American Earlier Black English: Morphological and Syntactic Variables* (Tuscaloosa: Univ. of Alabama Press, 1989), 145.
11. Cited in Schneider, *American Earlier English,* 148.
12. William C. Turner, Jr., foreword to *Sacred Symphony: The Chanted Sermon of the Black Preacher,* by Jon Michael Spencer (Westport, Conn.: Greenwood, 1987), xi.
13. Floyd, "On Integrative Inquiry," 5.

CHAPTER 1. THE RHYTHM

1. Laura M. Townes, Diary, 28 Apr. 1862, Penn School Papers, Southern Historical Collection, Univ. of North Carolina at Chapel Hill.
2. William Francis Allen, C. P. Ware, and L. M. Garrison, *Slave Songs of the United States* (1867; rpt. New York: Peter Smith, 1951), xiii–xiv.
3. John Paris, "The Moral and Religious Status of the African Race in the Southern States," MS, 13, Southern Historical Collection, Univ. of North Carolina at Chapel Hill.
4. Gerardus Van der Leeuw, *Sacred and Profane Beauty: The Holy in Art*, trans. David E. Green (London: Weidenfeld and Nicholson, 1963), 29.
5. Van der Leeuw, *Sacred and Profane Beauty*, 73.
6. Katrina Hazzard-Gordon, *Jookin': The Rise of Social Dance Formations in African-American Culture* (Philadelphia: Temple Univ. Press, 1990), 14.
7. Ibid., 18, 77.
8. Ibid., 81–82.
9. Ibid., 67, 80.
10. Ibid., 93.
11. Ibid., 84.
12. Ibid., 19, 87.
13. Ibid., 87.
14. Ibid., 159.
15. Ibid., 87, 210.
16. Alain L. Locke, "The American Negro as Artist," in *The Critical Temper of Alain Locke: A Selection of His Essays on Art and Culture*, ed. Jeffrey C. Stewart (New York: Garland, 1983), 171.
17. R. Nathaniel Dett, "Negro Music," in *The R. Nathaniel Dett Reader: Essays on Black Sacred Music*, ed. Jon Michael Spencer, special issue of *Black Sacred Music: A Journal of Theomusicology* 5, no. 2 (Fall 1991): 127.
18. William Grant Still, "The Music of My Race," translation in *The William Grant Still Reader: Essays on American Music*, ed. Jon Michael Spencer, special issue of *Black Sacred Music: A Journal of Theomusicology* 6, no. 2 (Fall 1992): 102.
19. See my extended argument in Jon Michael Spencer, *Blues and Evil* (Knoxville: Univ. of Tennessee Press, 1993), 120–37.
20. Alain L. Locke, "Youth Speaks," *Survey Graphic* 53, no. 11 (Mar. 1, 1925), in *The Critical Temper of Alain Locke*, 14.
21. Alain L. Locke, *The Negro and His Music* (Washington: The Associates in Negro Folk Education, 1936), 139–40.
22. Spencer, *Blues and Evil*, 120–37.
23. R. Nathaniel Dett, "From Bell Stand to Throne Room," in *The R. Nathaniel Dett Reader*, ed. Spencer, 97.
24. William Grant Still, "My Arkansas Boyhood," in *The William Grant Still Reader*, ed. Spencer, 248.
25. See the example in Jon Michael Spencer, *Sacred Symphony: The Chanted Sermon of the Black Preacher* (Westport. Conn.: Greenwood, 1987).
26. Van der Leeuw, *Sacred and Profane Beauty*, 234.

27. Cited in Anne Key Simpson, *Follow Me: The Life and Music of R. Nathaniel Dett* (Metuchen, N.J.: Scarecrow, 1993), 333.
28. Alain L. Locke to Charlotte Osgood Mason, 12 Mar. 1936, Alain L. Locke Papers, Manuscripts Department, Moorland-Spingarn Research Center, Howard Univ.
29. W. E. B. Du Bois, *Dusk of Dawn: An Essay Toward an Autobiography of a Race Concept* (New York: Harcourt, Brace, 1940), 117.
30. Sterling Stuckey, *Slave Culture: Nationalist Theory and the Foundations of Black America* (New York: Oxford Univ. Press, 1987), 17.
31. Van der Leeuw, *Sacred and Profane Beauty*, 49.
32. Ibid., 36.
33. Victor Turner, *The Ritual Process: Structure and Antistructure* (Ithaca, N.Y.: Cornell Univ. Press, 1969), 128.
34. I expound on this in Spencer, *Blues and Evil*, 6–13.
35. Martin Buber, *I and Thou*, trans. Ronald Gregor Smith (Edinburgh: T & T Clark, 1937), 95, 100, 116.
36. Bruce Reed, *The Dynamics of Religion: Process and Movement in Christian Churches* (London: Darton, Longman and Todd, 1978), 15, 32, 34, 35.
37. Langdon Gilkey, *Naming the Whirlwind: The Renewal of God-Language* (Indianapolis: Bobbs-Merrill, 1969), 248–49.
38. Leonard E. Barrett, *Soul-Force: African Heritage in Afro-American Religion* (Garden City, N.Y.: Anchor/Doubleday, 1974), 10.
39. Locke, *The Negro and His Music*, 139–40.
40. Leland Ferguson, *Uncommon Ground: Archaeology and Early African America, 1650–1800* (Washington: Smithsonian Institution Press, 1992), 123.
41. Martin Luther King, Jr., *Why We Can't Wait* (New York: Mentor, 1964), 61.
42. Van der Leeuw, *Sacred and Profane Beauty*, 115.
43. Ibid., 117.
44. Ibid., 124.
45. Carl E. Seashore, *Psychology of Music* (New York: McGraw-Hill, 1938), 142.
46. Van der Leeuw, *Sacred and Profane Beauty*, 28.
47. Kathleen Marie Higgins, *The Music of Our Lives* (Philadelphia: Temple Univ. Press, 1991), 154.
48. Ella Anderson Clark, "The Reminiscences of Ella Anderson Clark," MS, 43, James Osgood Andrew Clark Papers, Special Collections Department, Emory Univ.
49. Howard Odum and Guy B. Johnson, *The Negro and His Songs* (Hatboro, Penn.: Folklore Associates, 1964), 34.
50. Walter Fauntroy, "The Social Action Mission of the Church," taped lecture at Duke Univ. Divinity School, 22 Nov. 1981.
51. Van der Leeuw, *Sacred and Profane Beauty*, 73, 74.
52. Ibid., 42.
53. Ferguson, *Uncommon Ground*, xliv.
54. Ibid., 120.
55. Ibid., 117.

56. Barrett, *Soul-Force,* 83–84.
57. Paul Tillich, *Theology of Culture,* ed. Robert C. Kimball (New York: Oxford Univ. Press, 1959), 42.

CHAPTER 2. THE RELIGION

1. Robert Farris Thompson, *Flash of the Spirit: African and Afro-American Art and Philosophy* (New York: Vintage, 1983), xiii–xiv.
2. Ibid., 211.
3. Ibid., 207.
4. Ibid., 208.
5. Robert Farris Thompson, *African Art in Motion: Icon and Act* (Berkeley: Univ. of California Press, 1974), 13.
6. Donald J. Cosentino, "Interview with Robert Farris Thompson," *African Arts* 25, no. 4 (Oct. 1992): 55.
7. See Zora Neale Hurston, *Tell My Horse* (Berkeley, Calif.: Turtle Island, 1981), 137.
8. Paul Tillich, *Theology of Culture,* ed. Robert C. Kimball (New York: Oxford Univ. Press, 1959), 70.
9. Alan P. Merriam, *The Anthropology of Music* (Evanston, Ill.: Northwestern Univ. Press, 1964), 46.
10. Langdon Gilkey, *Society and the Sacred: Toward a Theology of Culture in Decline* (New York: Crossroad, 1981), 110.
11. Tillich, *Theology of Culture,* 41.
12. Ibid., 8.
13. Robert M. Shelton, "Doing Theology with Willie Nelson," in *Theomusicology,* ed. Jon Michael Spencer, special issue of *Black Sacred Music: A Journal of Theomusicology* 8, no. 1 (Spring 1994): 255–56.
14. Cited in Stephen Blum, "Prologue: Ethnomusicologists and Modern Music History," in *Ethnomusicology and Modern Music History,* eds. Stephen Blum, Philip V. Bohlman, and Daniel M. Neuman (Urbana: Univ. of Illinois Press, 1991), 2.
15. See Warren Dwight Allen, *Philosophies of Music History: A Study of General Histories of Music* (New York: Dover, 1962), 233.
16. Samuel A. Floyd, Jr., "On Integrative Inquiry: Toward a Common Scholarship," *CBMR Digest* 6, no. 1 (Winter 1993): 5.
17. See Jon Michael Spencer, *Theological Music: Introduction to Theomusicology* (Westport, Conn.: Greenwood, 1991), xi, 3–46. And see my introduction to *The Theology of American Popular Music,* ed. Jon Michael Spencer, special issue of *Black Sacred Music: A Journal of Theomusicology* 3, no. 2 (Fall 1989): 1–16.
18. Gerardus van der Leeuw, *Sacred and Profane Beauty: The Holy in Art,* trans. David E. Green (London: Weidenfeld and Nicholson, 1963), 246, 249.
19. Van der Leeuw, *Sacred and Profane Beauty,* 254.
20. Tillich, *Theology of Culture,* 42.
21. See Michael Goldberg, *Theology and Narrative: A Critical Introduction* (Nashville: Abingdon, 1981), 21, 34, 36, 37. Also see James W. McClendon, Jr., *Biography as Theology: How Life Stories Remake*

Today's Theology, new edition (Philadelphia: Trinity Press International, 1990).
22. James Clifford, "Introduction: Partial Truths," in *Writing Culture: The Poetics of Ethnography*, eds. James Clifford and George E. Marcus (Berkeley: Univ. of California Press, 1986), 14, 23.
23. Kathleen Marie Higgins, *The Music of Our Lives* (Philadelphia: Temple Univ. Press, 1991), 174.
24. Stephen A. Tyler, "Post-Modern Ethnography: From Document of the Occult to Occult Document," in *Writing Culture*, eds. Clifford and Marcus, 125, 126, 127, 129.
25. Ibid.,126, 130.
26. Philip V. Bohlman, "Is All Music Religious?" in *Theomusicology*, ed. Spencer, 11.
27. David Burrows, *Sound, Speech, and Music* (Amherst: Univ. of Massachusetts Press, 1990), 5.
28. Ibid., 6, 8.
29. Ibid., 8.
30. Ibid.
31. Ibid., 105.
32. Cited in Allen, *Philosophies of Music History*, 92.
33. Gilkey, *Society and the Sacred*, 62–63, 66.
34. Arthur Schopenhauer, *The World as Will and Representation*, vol. 1, trans. E. F. J. Payne (Indian Hills, Colo.: The Falcon's Wing Press, 1958), 257. Also see Friedrich Nietzsche, "The Birth of Tragedy from the Spirit of Music," trans. Clifton P. Fadiman, in *The Philosophy of Nietzsche* (New York: The Modern Library/Random House, 1927), 1037.
35. John Covach, "The Quest of the Absolute: Schoenberg, Hauer, and the Twelve-Tone Idea," in *Theomusicology*, ed. Spencer, 173–74.
36. Bruno Nettl, *Music in Primitive Culture* (Cambridge: Harvard Univ. Press, 1956), 104.

CHAPTER 3. FOLK MUSE

1. William C. Turner, Jr., foreword to Jon Michael Spencer, *Sacred Symphony: The Chanted Sermon of the Black Preacher* (Westport, Conn.: Greenwood, 1987), ix.
2. Ibid., x.
3. Ibid., x–xi.
4. Ibid., xi–xii.
5. See Henry Hugh Proctor, "The Theology of the Songs of the Southern Slave," *The Journal of Black Sacred Music* 2, no. 1 (Spring 1988): 51–64.
6. For a summary of this essay, see Jon Michael Spencer, *Theological Music: Introduction to Theomusicology* (Westport, Conn.: Greenwood, 1991), 7–10.
7. Paul Tillich, *Theology of Culture*, ed. Robert C. Kimball (New York: Oxford Univ. Press, 1959), 142–43.

8. Robert W. Gordon, "The Negro Spiritual," in *The Carolina Low-Country,* ed. Augustine T. Smythe, et al. (New York: Macmillan, 1932), 217.
9. Solomon Northup, *Twelve Years a Slave,* eds. Sue Eakin and Joseph Logsdon (Baton Rouge: Louisiana State Univ. Press, 1968), 158.
10. Frederick Douglass, *My Bondage and My Freedom* (New York: Dover, 1969), 99, 279.
11. James H. Cone, "Black Spirituals: A Theological Interpretation," *Theology Today* 29, no. 1 (Apr. 1972): 67.
12. James H. Cone, *God of the Oppressed* (New York: Seabury, 1975), 66.
13. Tillich, *Theology of Culture,* 29.
14. Vincent L. Wimbush, "Biblical Historical Study as Liberation: Toward an Afro-Christian Hermeneutic," in *African American Religious Studies: An Interdisciplinary Anthology,* ed. Gayraud S. Wilmore (Durham, N.C.: Duke Univ. Press, 1989), 144–45.
15. Ibid., 152.
16. Henry H. Mitchell and Nicholas Cooper-Lewter, *Soul Theology: The Heart of American Black Culture* (San Francisco: Harper and Row, 1986), 4.
17. Ibid., 17–18.
18. Ibid., 4, 167.
19. Ibid., 4.
20. Ibid., 3.
21. Ibid., 6.
22. See Jon Michael Spencer, *Blues and Evil* (Knoxville: Univ. of Tennessee Press, 1993).
23. James H. Cone, *The Spirituals and the Blues: An Introduction* (San Francisco: Harper and Row, 1972), 125–26.
24. Houston A. Baker, Jr., *Blues, Ideology, and Afro-American Literature: A Vernacular Theory* (Chicago: Univ. of Chicago Press, 1984), 1–14.
25. Henry Louis Gates, Jr., *The Signifying Monkey: A Theory of Afro-American Literary Criticism* (New York: Oxford Univ. Press, 1988), xix–xxviii.
26. John A. Burrison, ed., *Storytellers: Folktales and Legends from the South* (Athens: Univ. of Georgia Press, 1989), 1.
27. Told by Bill Emmett, in Burrison, ed., *Storytellers,* 176.
28. See C. G. Jung, "On the Psychology of the Trickster Figure," postscript to Paul Radin, *The Trickster: A Study in American Indian Mythology* (London: Routledge and Kegan Paul, 1956), 195–211.
29. John A. Sanford, "The Problem of Evil in Christianity and Analytical Psychology," in *Carl Jung and Christian Spirituality,* ed. Robert L. Moore (New York: Paulist Press, 1988), 129–30.
30. David Evans, "The Rev. Rubin Lacy" (interview), *Blues Unlimited,* 43 (May 1967): 13.
31. Clyde J. Steckel, "How Can Music Have Theological Significance?" in *Theomusicology,* ed. Jon Michael Spencer, special issue of *Black Sacred Music: A Journal of Theomusicology* 8, no. 1 (Spring 1994): 14.

CHAPTER 4. POPULAR MUSE

1. Samuel A. Floyd, Jr., "On Integrative Inquiry: Toward a Common Scholarship," *CBMR Digest* 6, no. 1 (Winter 1993): 1.
2. Kathleen Marie Higgins, *The Music of Our Lives* (Philadelphia: Temple Univ. Press, 1991), 29.
3. Paul Tillich, *Theology of Culture*, ed. Robert C. Kimball (New York: Oxford Univ. Press, 1959), 12–13.
4. Angela M. S. Nelson, "Text, Texture, and Context in Theological Perspective," in *Theomusicology*, ed. Jon Michael Spencer, special issue of *Black Sacred Music: A Journal of Theomusicology* 8, no. 1 (Spring 1994): 73.
5. Nelson, "Text, Texture, and Context in Theological Perspective," 73.
6. Philip M. Royster, "The Rapper as Shaman for a Band of Dancers of the Spirit: 'U Can't Touch This,'" in *The Emergency of Black and the Emergence of Rap*, ed. Jon Michael Spencer, special issue of *Black Sacred Music: A Journal of Theomusicology* 5, no. 1 (Spring 1991): 61.
7. Mark Sumner Harvey, "Rhythm, Ritual, and Religion: Postmodern (Musical) Agonistes," in *Theomusicology*, ed. Spencer, 193–94.
8. Gerardus van der Leeuw, *Sacred and Profane Beauty: The Holy in Art*, trans. David E. Green (London: Weidenfeld and Nicholson, 1963), 278–79.
9. Clyde J. Steckel, "How Can Music Have Theological Significance?" in *Theomusicology*, ed. Spencer, 14.
10. Bernd Schwarze, "Religion, Rock, and Research," in *Theomusicology*, ed. Spencer, 90.
11. Jon Michael Spencer, *Theological Music: Introduction to Theomusicology* (Westport, Conn: Greenwood, 1991), 4–5.
12. Higgins, *The Music of Our Lives*, 71. Emphasis added.
13. N. Lynne Westfield and Harold Dean Trulear, "Theomusicology and Christian Education: Spirituality and the Ethics of Control in the Rap of Hammer," in *Theomusicology*, ed. Spencer, 221.
14. Westfield and Trulear, "Theomusicology and Christian Education," 219–20.
15. Lucius C. Harper, "We Prefer the 'Blues' to Our Essential Causes," *The Chicago Defender*, 1 Oct. 1938, 16.
16. Cited in *History of Church of Christ (Holiness) U.S.A.*, ed. Otho B. Cobbins (New York: Vantage Press, 1966), 407.
17. See Charles Price Jones's gospel hymns "The Time Will Not Be Long," "None But Christ," "I Will Hide," "Precious Savior."
18. See Charles Albert Tindley's gospel hymns "Some Day" and "After a While."
19. Alexander L. Jackson, "The Onlooker" (column), *The Chicago Defender*, 14 Jan. 1922, pt. 2, 4.
20. Robert S. Abbott, "Refinement Sadly Lacking in Modern Youth," *The Chicago Defender*, 10 Mar. 1934, 11.
21. E. Elliott Rawlins, "The Intoxication of Jazz," *The New York Amsterdam News*, 11 Apr. 1923, 12.
22. E. Elliott Rawlins, "Jazz—a Drug," *The New York Amsterdam News*, 1 Apr. 1925, 16.

23. See Thomas A. Dorsey's gospel songs "Tell Jesus Everything" and "Someday, Somewhere."
24. Leonard E. Barrett, *Soul-Force: African Heritage in Afro-American Religion* (Garden City, N.Y.: Anchor/Doubleday, 1974), 1.
25. "Divinity Prof: Prince's Music Touches on the Spiritual," *The Durham Sun,* 4 Mar. 1989, C-1.
26. "Groovin' on Gleaning—Guardedly," *The United Methodist Reporter,* 7 Apr. 1989, 2.
27. Tipper Gore, "Hate, Rape and Rap," *Washington Post,* Jan. 8, 1990, 15A.
28. George F. Will, "America's Slide into the Sewer," *Newsweek,* July 30, 1990, 64.
29. "NYC Crime: 3 Teens Get Prison for Assault of Jogger," *USA Today,* 12 Sept. 1990, 2A.
30. Westfield and Trulear, "Theomusicology and Christian Education," 219.
31. The proceedings were published in *The Theology of American Popular Music,* ed. Jon Michael Spencer, special issue of *Black Sacred Music: A Journal of Theomusicology* 3, no. 2 (Fall 1989).
32. Jon Michael Spencer, "God in Secular Music Culture: The Theodicy of the Blues as the Paradigm of Proof," in *The Theology of American Popular Music,* ed. Spencer, 18.
33. Hugh J. Roberts, "Improvisation, Individuation, and Immanence: Thelonius Monk," in *The Theology of American Popular Music,* ed. Spencer, 51.
34. Ibid., 51–52.
35. Ibid., 55.
36. Earlston E. DeSilva, "The Theology of Black Power and Black Song: James Brown," in *The Theology of American Popular Music,* ed. Spencer, 59–60.
37. Ibid., 61.
38. Ibid., 65.
39. Alton B. Pollard, III, "The Last Soul Singer in America: Al Green," in *The Theology of American Popular Music,* ed. Spencer, 87–88.
40. Pollard, "The Last Soul Singer in America," 96–97.
41. Orea Jones, "The Theology of 'Sexual Healing': Marvin Gaye," in *The Theology of American Popular Music,* ed. Spencer, 69.
42. Ibid., 70.
43. Richard E. Wimberley, "Prophecy, Eroticism, and Apocalypticism in Popular Music: Prince," in *The Theology of American Popular Music,* ed. Spencer, 130.
44. Alton B. Pollard III, "Religion, Rock, and Eroticism: Prince," in *The Theology of American Popular Music,* ed. Spencer, 139.
45. Harold Dean Trulear, "The Prophetic Character of Black Secular Music: Stevie Wonder," in *The Theology of American Popular Music,* ed. Spencer, 76.
46. Michael Eric Dyson, "A Postmodern Afro-American Secular Spirituality: Michael Jackson," in *The Theology of American Popular Music,* ed. Spencer, 102.

47. Ibid., 98.
48. Ibid., 105.

CHAPTER 5. CLASSICAL MUSE

1. Gerardus van der Leeuw, *Sacred and Profane Beauty: The Holy in Art,* trans. David E. Green (London: Weidenfeld and Nicholson, 1963), 35, 55–56, 74.
2. Natalie Curtis, ed., *The Indians' Book* (New York: Harper and Brothers, 1907), xxi, xxiii.
3. Ibid., xxx.
4. Albert C. Barnes, "Negro Art and America," in *The New Negro,* ed. Alain L. Locke (New York: Atheneum, 1980 [1925]), 19, 20, 23, 24, 25.
5. Charlotte Osgood Mason, notebooks, 20 Feb. 1927, Alain Locke Papers, Manuscripts Department, Moorland-Spingarn Research Center, Howard Univ.
6. Mason, notebook, 10 and 17 Mar. 1927, Locke Papers.
7. Langston Hughes to Locke, n.d., 1928, Locke Papers.
8. Langston Hughes, *The Big Sea* (New York: Hill and Wang, 1940), 325.
9. Alain Locke, *The Negro and His Music* (Washington, D.C.: The Associates in Negro Folk Education, 1936), 139–40.
10. Olin Downes, "Hampton Institute Choir," *The New York Times,* 18 Apr. 1928.
11. Ibid.
12. Olin Downes, "Cincinnati Hears Music by Berlioz; Dett Piece Also Is Heard," *The New York Times,* 8 May 1937, 22.
13. Olin Downes, "Ballet Presented at Rochester Fete," *The New York Times,* 24 May 1931.
14. John Covach, "The Quest of the Absolute: Schoenberg, Hauer, and the Twelve-Tone Idea," in *Theomusicology,* ed. Jon Michael Spencer, special issue of *Black Sacred Music: A Journal of Theomusicology* 8, no. 1 (Spring 1994): 159, 165–66.
15. William Grant Still, Autobiography, MS, 166, n.d., William Grant Still and Verna Arvey Papers, Special Collections Division, Univ. of Arkansas Library, Fayetteville.
16. Cited in J. Douglas Cook, "Visits to the Homes of Famous Composers: No. 3, William Grant Still," *Opera, Concert and Symphony,* Nov. 1946, 9.
17. William Grant Still, "The Art of Musical Creation," in *The William Grant Still Reader: Essays on American Music,* ed. Jon Michael Spencer, special issue of *Black Sacred Music: A Journal of Theomusicology* 6, no. 2 (Fall 1992): 82.
18. Verna Arvey, "What Can They Tell Us, Those Spirits Who Have Never Been Incarnate?" MS, 1, 5, Still-Arvey Papers.
19. WW meeting transcript, Feb. 8, 1958, Still-Arvey Papers.
20. The above biographical material on Lange is from Arvey, "What Can They Tell Us, Those Spirits Who Have Never Been Incarnate?" 8.
21. Ibid., 1.
22. Ibid.

23. Ibid., 2, 3.
24. WW meeting transcript, 9 Jan. 1955.
25. William Grant Still, "The Seven Wonders: The Wonder of Music," MS, 27 Sept. 1964, 1, Still-Arvey Papers.
26. Ibid.
27. Ibid., 1–2.
28. Ibid., 2–3.
29. Ibid., 3.
30. WW meeting transcript, 3 Apr. 1966.
31. WW meeting transcript, 8 Sept. 1958.
32. Robert A. Martin, interview with William Grant Still, MS, May 1964, 12, Still-Arvey Papers.
33. William Grant Still, "The Composer Needs Determination and Faith," in *The William Grant Still Reader,* ed. Spencer, 167.
34. Ibid., 168.
35. Still, "The Composer's Creed," in *The William Grant Still Reader,* ed. Spencer, 199.
36. William Grant Still, Diary, 2 Mar. 1951, Still-Arvey Papers.
37. Verna Arvey, *In One Lifetime* (Fayetteville: Univ. of Arkansas Press, 1984), 174.
38. Ibid.
39. Still, "A Composer's Viewpoint," in *The William Grant Still Reader,* ed. Spencer, 226.
40. WW meeting transcript, 11 Feb. 1965. See also 16 Oct. 1966.
41. Ibid., 1 Dec. 1963. Also quoted in Arvey, "What Can They Tell Us, Those Spirits Who Have Never Been Incarnate?" 4.
42. Still, Autobiography, 308.
43. WW meeting transcript, 3 Dec. 1955. Also quoted in Arvey, "What Can They Tell Us, Those Spirits Who Have Never Been Incarnate?" 6.
44. WW meeting transcript, 17 Dec. 1977.
45. Ibid., 14 Sept. 1956.
46. Eva May Carrell reading transcript, 29 Oct. 1967, Still-Arvey Papers.
47. WW meeting transcript, 26 Jan. 1963.
48. Ibid., 3 Apr. 1966.
49. Ibid., 25 Jan.1960.
50. Arvey, "What Can They Tell Us, Those Spirits Who Have Never Been Incarnate?" 6.
51. WW meeting transcript, 4 Mar. 1962.
52. Ibid., 14 Sept. 1956; 20 July 1958.
53. William Grant Still, Presentation on *The Peaceful Land,* MS, 22 Oct. 1961, 1, Still-Arvey Papers.
54. William Grant Still, "The Composer Needs Determination and Faith," 168.

CHAPTER 6. AN ETHICS

1. N. Lynne Westfield and Harold Dean Trulear, "Theomusicology and Christian Education: Spirituality and the Ethics of Control in the Rap of Hammer," in *Theomusicology,* ed. Jon Michael Spencer, special issue of

Black Sacred Music: A Journal of Theomusicology 8, no. 1 (Spring 1994): 219–20.
2. Ibid., 237.
3. Ibid., 236–37.
4. David Evans, "The Rev. Rubin Lacy" (interview), *Blues Unlimited* 43 (May 1967): 13.
5. Samuel A. Floyd, Jr., "On Integrative Inquiry: Toward a Common Scholarship," *CBMR Digest* 6, no. 1 (Winter 1993): 1.
6. Paul Oliver, *Blues Fell This Morning: Meaning in the Blues*, 2nd ed. (Cambridge: Cambridge Univ. Press, 1990), 118.
7. Floyd, "On Integrative Inquiry," 1.
8. David Burrows to Jon Michael Spencer, MS, 29 Dec. 1990.
9. David Burrows, *Sound, Speech, and Music* (Amherst: Univ. of Massachusetts Press, 1990), 95.
10. Ellen Koskoff, "An Introduction to Women, Music, and Culture," in *Women and Music in Cross-Cultural Perspective*, ed. Ellen Koskoff (Urbana: Univ. of Illinois Press, 1989), 1.
11. L. JaFran Jones, "A Sociohistorical Perspective on Tunisian Women as Professional Musicians," in *Women and Music*, ed. Koskoff, 69–70. Emphasis added.
12. Ibid., 82.
13. Carol E. Robertson, "Power and Gender in the Musical Experiences of Women," in *Women and Music,* ed. Koskoff, 225, 227.
14. Ibid., 229–30.
15. Ibid., 238.
16. J. Michael Jarrett, "On Jazzology: A Rhapsody," in *Sacred Music of the Secular City,* ed. Jon Michael Spencer, special issue of *Black Sacred Music: A Journal of Theomusicology* 6:1 (Spring 1992): 199.
17. Ibid., 177–80.
18. Ibid., 200.
19. Daniel M. Neuman, "Epilogue: Paradigms and Stories," in *Ethnomusicology and Modern Music History,* eds. Stephen Blum, Philip V. Bohlman, and Daniel M. Neuman (Urbana: Univ. of Illinois Press, 1991), 269–70.
20. Ibid., 269.
21. Ibid.
22. Helen Bruch Pearson, "The Battered Bartered Bride," *The Hymn* 34 (Oct. 1983): 216.
23. See the biblical exegesis I do on this passage in Jon Michael Spencer, *Sing a New Song: Liberating Black Hymnody* (Minneapolis: Fortress, 1995), 85–114.
24. Cornel West, *The American Evasion of Philosophy: A Genealogy of Pragmatism* (Madison: Univ. of Wisconsin Press, 1989), 230.
25. Ibid., 212.
26. Ibid., 212, 239.
27. Clyde J. Steckel, "How Can Music Have Theological Significance?" in *Theomusicology,* ed. Spencer, 22.
28. Houston A. Baker, Jr., *Blues, Ideology, and Afro-American Literature: A Vernacular Theory* (Chicago: Univ. of Chicago Press, 1984), 10.

29. Ibid., 115.
30. Molefi Kete Asante, *Kemet, Afrocentricity and Knowledge* (Trenton: Africa World Press, 1990), 107, 108, 109.
31. West, *American Evasion of Philosophy*, 110.
32. Donald J. Cosentino, "Interview with Robert Farris Thompson," *African Arts* 25:4 (Oct. 1992): 62.
33. Stanley M. Hauerwas, *Christian Existence Today: Essays on Church, World and Living in Between* (Durham, N.C.: Labyrinth Press, 1988), vii.
34. See Jon Michael Spencer, *Theological Music: Introduction to Theomusicology* (Westport, Conn.: Greenwood, 1991), xiv.
35. Terry E. Miller, review of *Sacred Music of the Secular City*, ed. Jon Michael Spencer, *The Hymn* 44, no. 1 (Jan. 1993): 46.
36. Warren Dwight Allen, *Philosophies of Music History: A Study of General Histories of Music* (New York: Dover, 1962), 14, 18.
37. Langdon Gilkey, *Society and the Sacred: Toward a Theology of Culture in Decline* (New York: Crossroad, 1981), 81.
38. Ibid., 84.
39. Nicholas Cooper-Lewter, "Keep Rollin' Along: The Temptations and Soul Therapy," in *Sacred Music of the Secular City*, ed. Spencer, 219–20.
40. William C. Turner, Jr., "Keep On Pushing: The Impressions," in *Sacred Music of the Secular City*, ed. Spencer, 208.
41. Cooper-Lewter, "Keep On Rollin' Along," 222.
42. Martin Buber, *I and Thou*, trans. Ronald Gregor Smith (Edinburgh: T & T Clark, 1937), 95, 100, 116.
43. Bruce Reed, *The Dynamics of Religion: Process and Movement in Christian Churches* (London: Darton, Longman and Todd, 1978), 15, 32, 34, 35.
44. Cooper-Lewter, "Keep On Rollin' Along," 222–23.
45. Paul Tillich, *Theology of Culture*, ed. Robert C. Kimball (New York: Oxford Univ. Press, 1959), 114.

CONCLUSION

1. Told by Lee Drake, in *Storytellers: Folktales and Legends from the South*, ed. John A. Burrison (Athens: Univ. of Georgia Press, 1989), 110–11.
2. James R. Aswell, et al., eds., *God Bless the Devil!: Liar's Bench Tales* (Chapel Hill: Univ. of North Carolina Press, 1940), xi.
3. John S. Mbiti, *African Religions and Philosophy* (Garden City, N.Y.: Anchor/Doubleday, 1970), 31–34.
4. Sterling Stuckey, *Slave Culture: Nationalist Theory and the Foundations of Black America* (New York: Oxford Univ. Press, 1987), 17.

SELECT BIBLIOGRAPHY

Allen, Warren Dwight. *Philosophies of Music History: A Study of General Histories of Music.* New York: Dover, 1962.
Allen, William Francis, C. P. Ware, and L. M. Garrison. *Slave Songs of the United States.* 1867. Rpt. New York: Peter Smith, 1951.
Arvey, Verna. *In One Lifetime.* Fayetteville: Univ. of Arkansas Press, 1984.
Asante, Molefi Kete. *The Afrocentric Idea.* Philadelphia: Temple Univ. Press, 1987.
———. *Kemet, Afrocentricity and Knowledge.* (Trenton: Africa World Press, 1990.
Baker, Houston A., Jr. *Blues, Ideology, and Afro-American Literature: A Vernacular Theory.* Chicago: Univ. of Chicago Press, 1984.
Barrett, Leonard E. *Soul-Force: African Heritage in Afro-American Religion.* Garden City, N.Y.: Anchor/Doubleday, 1974.
Blum, Stephen, Philip V. Bohlman, and Daniel M. Neuman, eds. *Ethnomusicology and Modern Music History.* Urbana: Univ. of Illinois Press, 1991.
Burrows, David. *Sound, Speech, and Music.* Amherst: Univ. of Massachusetts Press, 1990.
Clifford, James, and George E. Marcus, eds. *Writing Culture: The Poetics of Ethnography.* Berkeley: Univ. of California Press, 1986.
Cone, James H. *God of the Oppressed.* New York: Seabury, 1975,
———. *The Spirituals and the Blues: An Interpretation.* San Francisco: Harper and Row, 1972.
Cooper-Lewter, Nicholas, and Henry H. Mitchell. *Soul Theology: The Heart of American Black Culture.* San Francisco: Harper and Row, 1986.
Cosentino, Donald J. "Interview with Robert Farris Thompson." *African Arts* 25, no. 4 (Oct. 1992): 52–63.
Dett, R. Nathaniel. *The R. Nathaniel Dett Reader: Essays on Black Sacred Music,* ed. Jon Michael Spencer. Special issue of *Black Sacred Music: A Journal of Theomusicology* 5, no. 2 (Fall 1991).
Eliade, Mircea. *The Sacred and the Profane: The Nature of Religion.* New York: Harcourt Brace and World, 1959.
———. *Symbolism, the Sacred, and the Arts,* ed. Diane Apostolos-Cappadona. New York: Crossroad, 1988.

Ferguson, Leland. *Uncommon Ground: Archaeology and Early African America, 1650–1800.* Washington: Smithsonian Institution Press, 1992.

Finn, Julio. *The Bluesman: The Musical Heritage of Black Men and Women in the Americas.* London: Quartet, 1986.

Floyd, Samuel A., Jr. "On Integrative Inquiry: Toward a Common Scholarship." *CBMR Digest* 6, no. 1 (Winter 1993): 1–6.

———. "'Ring Shout!' Literary Studies, Historical Studies, and Black Music Inquiry." *Black Music Research Journal* 11, no. 2 (Fall 1991): 265–87.

Gates, Henry Louis, Jr. *The Signifying Monkey: A Theory of Afro-American Literary Criticism.* New York: Oxford Univ. Press, 1988.

George, Nelson. *The Death of Rhythm and Blues.* New York: Pantheon, 1988.

Gilkey, Langdon. *Naming the Whirlwind: The Renewal of God-Language.* Indianapolis: Bobbs-Merrill, 1969.

———. *Society and the Sacred: Toward a Theology of Culture in Decline.* New York: Crossroad, 1981.

Goldberg, Michael. *Theology and Narrative: A Critical Introduction.* Nashville: Abingdon, 1981.

Greeley, Andrew. *God in Popular Culture.* Chicago: Thomas More, 1988.

Guralnick, Peter. *Searching for Robert Johnson.* New York: Dutton, 1989.

———. *Sweet Soul Music: Rhythm and Blues and the Southern Dream of Freedom.* New York: Harper and Row, 1986.

Hazzard-Gordon, Katrina. *Jookin': The Rise of Social Dance Formations in African-American Culture.* Philadelphia: Temple Univ. Press, 1990.

Higgins, Kathleen Marie. *The Music of Our Lives.* Philadelphia: Temple Univ. Press, 1991.

Holloway, Joseph E., ed. *Africanisms in American Culture.* Bloomington: Indiana Univ. Press, 1990.

Jones, LeRoi. *Black Music.* New York: William Morrow, 1969.

———. *Blues People: Negro Music in White America.* New York: William Morrow, 1963.

Jung, C. G. "On the Psychology of the Trickster Figure." Postscript to *The Trickster: A Study in American Indian Mythology,* by Paul Radin. London: Routledge and Kegan Paul, 1956.

Koskoff, Ellen, ed. *Women and Music in Cross-Cultural Perspective.* Urbana: Univ. of Illinois Press, 1936.

Leonard, Neil. *Jazz: Myth and Religion.* New York: Oxford Univ. Press, 1987.

Locke, Alain L. *The Negro and His Music.* Washington, D.C.: The Associates in Negro Folk Education, 1936.

Mbiti, John S. *African Religions and Philosophy.* Garden City, N.Y.: Anchor/Doubleday, 1970.

McClendon, James W., Jr. *Biography as Theology: How Life Stories Remake Today's Theology.* New ed. Philadelphia: Trinity Press International, 1990.

Merriam, Alan P. *The Anthropology of Music.* Evanston, Ill.: Northwestern Univ. Press, 1964.

Moore, Robert L., ed. *Carl Jung and Christian Spirituality.* New York: Paulist Press, 1988.

Nettl, Bruno. *Music in Primitive Culture*. Cambridge: Harvard Univ. Press, 1956.
Nietzsche, Friedrich. "The Birth of Tragedy from the Spirit of Music." Trans. by Clifton P. Fadiman. In *The Philosophy of Nietzsche*. New York: The Modern Library/Random House, 1927.
Ogren, Kathy J. *The Jazz Revolution: Twenties America and the Meaning of Jazz*. New York: Oxford Univ. Press, 1989.
Oliver, Paul. *Blues Fell This Morning: Meaning in the Blues*. 2d Ed. Cambridge: Cambridge Univ. Press, 1990.
―――. *Conversation with the Blues*. New York: Horizon, 1965.
Pelton, Robert D. *The Trickster in West Africa: A Study of Mythic Irony and Sacred Delight*. Berkeley: Univ. of California Press, 1980.
Proctor, Henry Hugh. "The Theology of the Songs of the Southern Slave." *The Journal of Black Sacred Music* 2, no. 1 (Spring 1988): 51–64. First published in *Southern Workman* 36 (1907): 584–92, 652–56.
Reed, Bruce. *The Dynamics of Religion: Process and Movement in Christian Churches*. London: Darton, Longman and Todd, 1978.
Roberts, John W. *From Trickster to Badman: The Black Folk Hero in Slavery and Freedom*. Philadelphia: Univ. of Pennsylvania Press, 1989.
Schopenhauer, Arthur. *The World as Will and Representation*. Vol. 1. Trans. by E. F. J. Payne. Indian Hills, Colo.: The Falcon's Wing Press, 1958.
Seashore, Carl E. *Psychology of Music*. New York: McGraw-Hill, 1938.
Simpson, Anne Key. *Follow Me: The Life and Music of R. Nathaniel Dett*. Metuchen, N.J.: Scarecrow, 1993.
Spencer, Jon Michael. *Blues and Evil*. Knoxville: Univ. of Tennessee Press, 1993.
―――, ed. *The Emergency of Black and the Emergence of Rap*. Special issue of *Black Sacred Music: A Journal of Theomusicology* 5, no. 1 (Spring 1991).
―――. *Protest and Praise: Sacred Music of Black Religion*. Minneapolis: Fortress, 1990.
―――, ed. *The R. Nathaniel Dett Reader: Essays on Black Sacred Music*. Special issue of *Black Sacred Music: A Journal of Theomusicology* 5, no. 2 (Fall 1991).
―――. *The Rhythms of Black Folks: Race, Religion, and Pan-Africanism*. Trenton, N.J.: Africa World, 1994.
―――, ed. *Sacred Music of the Secular City: From Blues to Rap*. Special issue of *Black Sacred Music: A Journal of Theomusicology* 6, no. 1 (Spring 1992).
―――. *Sacred Symphony: The Chanted Sermon of the Black Preacher*. Westport, Conn.: Greenwood, 1987.
―――. *Sing a New Song: Liberating Black Hymnody*. Minneapolis: Fortress, 1994.
―――. *Theological Music: Introduction to Theomusicology*. Westport, Conn.: Greenwood, 1991.
―――, ed. *The Theology of American Popular Music*. Special issue of *Black Sacred Music: A Journal of Theomusicology* 3, no. 2 (Fall 1989).
―――, ed. *Theomusicology*. Special issue of *Black Sacred Music: A Journal of Theomusicology* 8, no. 1 (Spring 1994).

———, ed. *The William Grant Still Reader: Essays on American Music*. Special issue of *Black Sacred Music: A Journal of Theomusicology* 6, no. 2 (Fall 1992).

Stewart, Jeffrey C., ed. *The Critical Temper of Alain Locke: A Selection of His Essays on Art and Culture*. New York: Garland, 1983.

Still, William Grant. *The William Grant Still Reader: Essays on American Music*, ed. Jon Michael Spencer. Special issue of *Black Sacred Music: A Journal of Theomusicology* 6, no. 2 (Fall 1992).

Stuckey, Sterling. *Going through the Storm: The Influence of African American Art in History*. New York: Oxford Univ. Press, 1994.

———. *Slave Culture: Nationalist Theory and the Foundations of Black America*. New York: Oxford Univ. Press, 1987.

Thompson, Robert Farris. *African Art in Motion: Icon and Act*. Berkeley: Univ. of California Press, 1974.

———. *Flash of the Spirit: African and Afro-American Art and Philosophy*. New York: Vintage, 1983.

Tillich, Paul. *Theology of Culture*. Ed. Robert C. Kimball. New York: Oxford Univ. Press, 1959.

Turner, Victor. *The Ritual Process: Structure and Antistructure*. Ithaca, N.Y.: Cornell Univ. Press, 1969.

Van der Leeuw, Gerardus. *Sacred and Profane Beauty: The Holy in Art*. Trans. David E. Green. London: Weidenfeld and Nicolson, 1963.

West, Cornel. *The American Evasion of Philosophy: A Genealogy of Pragmatism*. Madison: Univ. of Wisconsin Press, 1989.

UNPUBLISHED PAPERS

Clark, James Osgood Andrew. Papers. Special Collections Department, Emory Univ.

Locke, Alain L. Papers. Manuscripts Department, Moorland-Spingarn Research Center, Howard Univ.

Townes, Laura M. Penn School Papers. Southern Historical Collection, Univ. of North Carolina at Chapel Hill.

Still, William Grant and Verna Arvey. Papers. Special Collections Division, Univ. of Arkansas Library, Fayetteville.

INDEX

a-, preverbal, 4–5
Abbott, Robert, 76
African dance styles, 13–14
African music: as influence on black art criticism, 31–33
African rhythms, 11–12, 15–16, 22; and archaeological evidence, 27–28; of black preaching, 17; impact of on black culture, 27–29; religious role of, 21, 28–29, 32–33; role of in African cultures, 6
African textiles: musical aspects of, 31
Ailey, Alvin, 6
Ali, Muhammad, 7
Anderson, Marian, 7, 15, 92
Arvey, Verna, 97, 101
Asante, Molefi, 118–19
Aswell, James, 129–30

Baker, Houston, Jr., 6, 59, 118
Baraka, Amiri, 32
Barnes, Albert C., 90, 91
Barrett, Leonard, 22, 28, 79
Battle, Kathleen, 7
Bernstein, Leonard, 101
Bible: and re-searching black music, 56–57, 72–73
black church: and black music, 130–33; and the blues, xiii–xvii
black culture: white views of, 90–95
black literature: linkages with black music, 3, 6–7
black music, re-search of: best approach to, 1–9; Bible as relevant to, 56–57, 72–73; classical composers, 93–106; common mode of inquiry, 2–8; culture-derived elements, 1–2; linkages with black literature, 3, 6–7; need for sexual ethic, 108–9; social sciences applied to, 37–39; spirituality of, 132–33; theomusicology as approach to, 36–37, 44–46, 50–59, 120; white views of, 93–94. *See also* popular music
black preaching: and the blues, 61–62, 63; correlation with spirituals, 47–48; as kratophany, 49; musicality of, 48–50
Blake, Eubie, 100
blues: and African cosmology, 130–31; perceptions of, 74–75, 109–10; and rap, 69; relationship with church, xiii–xvii; religious aspects of, 58–59, 61–62, 63; secular offspring of, 82–83; and spirituals, 57; Still's view of, 99
blues singers: sexual ethic of, 109; sexuality of, 61
Bohlman, Philip, 42
Broonzy, Big Bill, xvii, 109
Brown, James, 6, 78, 79, 83–84
Buber, Martin, 21, 123–24
Burrison, John, 60
Burrows, David, 42, 48, 68, 110
Butler, Jerry, 122

camel walk (dance), 14
Carrell, Eva May, 103
Chapman, Tracy, 7
Charles, Ray, 78
The Chicago Defender, 76
church. *See* black church; religion
civil rights movement, 27
Clark, Dave, 78
Clark, Ella, 26
classical music, 93–106

Comte, August, 37, 42–43
Cone, James H., 51, 52, 53, 54–55, 56
Cooke, Sam, 78
Cooper-Lewter, Nicholas, 39–40, 51, 57, 58, 120–21; "soul therapy" of, 121–22, 123, 124–25, 126
Cornelius, Stephen, 39, 120–21
Covach, John, 43–44
Curtis, King, 78
Curtis, Natalie, 90, 91

dance styles: African origins of, 13–14
Davis, Chuck, 6
DeSilva, Earlston, 83–84
Dett, R. Nathaniel, 7, 15, 16, 18, 29, 93, 94
Dewey, John, 117
Dorsey, Thomas, 78
Douglass, Frederick, 7, 53
Downes, Olin, 93–94, 99, 106
Drake, Lee, 129
drums: importance of in African society, 11–12, 15, 23
Du Bois, W. E. B., 18, 117
Dunbar, Paul Laurence, 3
Dvořák, Antonin, 16
Dyson, Michael Eric, 86–87

Early Jazz (Schuller), 114
Edwin Hawkins Singers, 79
Eliade, Mircea, 51
Emerson, Ralph Waldo, 117
ethnography: postmodern, 41; self-reflexivity in, 40–41
ethnomusicology, 35–37, 110–13

Fauntroy, Walter, 26–27
Feagin, Crawford, 4
Ferguson, Leland, 23–24, 28
Fitzgerald, Ella, 6
Flash of the Spirit: African and Afro-American Art and Philosophy (Thompson), 30
Floyd, Samuel, Jr., 1–2, 31, 37, 66, 109, 110
Franklin, Aretha, 78

Gates, Henry Louis, Jr., 6, 59–60
Gaye, Marvin, 79, 85
Genesis, 115–16
Gilkey, Langdon, 21, 34–35, 43, 120
"Go Down, Moses," 54
Gordon, Robert, 52–53, 57

Gore, Tipper, 80
gospel music, 79
Green, Al, 79, 84

"Hallelujah, I Love Her So," 78
Hammer (rap artist), 6, 69, 72, 108
Handy, W. C., 100
Hanslick, Eduard, 65
Harper, Lucius, 74–75
Harris, Michael, 5
Harvey, Mark Sumner, 69–70
Hauer, Josef Matthias, 95
Hauerwas, Stanley, 119
Havens, Richie, 6
Hayes, Roland, 15, 18
Hazzard-Gordon, Katrina, 29
heaven: as viewed in black music, 130–31
Higgins, Kathleen, 25, 41, 71
House, Son, xvii, 130
"Howling Wolf Blues," 130
Hughes, Langston, 91, 92–93
Hurston, Zora Neale, 91

Ice T., 81
Impressions, 122
The Indians' Book (Curtis), 90–91
itch (dance), 14

Jackson, Alexander, 76
Jackson, Jesse, 22
Jackson, Michael, 6, 79, 80, 86, 87
James, William, 117
Jarrett, Michael, 113–14
jazz: criticism of, 113–14; as dangerous music, 75–77
Johnson, Charles, 6
Johnson, Guy B., 26
Johnson, Robert, xvii, 6, 61
Johnson, Samuel, 119
Jones, Charles Price, 75
Jones, JaFran, 111–12, 117
Jones, Orea, 85
jook joints, 13–14
Jung, C. G., 51–52, 82; concept of "the Self," 62

Kant, Immanuel, 44, 65
Kincaid, Jamaica, 6
King, Martin Luther, Jr., 22, 24, 27
Kool Moe Dee, 69
Koskoff, Ellen, 111–12

Index

Lacy, Rubin, 61, 63, 109, 131
Lange, Arthur, 97
Lange, Marjorie, 97–98
Lawrence, Jacob, 7
Leadbelly, 61
Locke, Alain, 14, 23, 29, 91, 93
The Lost Continent (Still), 104

Mason, Charlotte Osgood, 90–91, 99, 105–6; views of black culture, 92
Mayfield, Curtis, 122
Maynor, Dorothy, 15, 18
McKay, Claude, 92
McMillan, Terry, 6
Merriam, Alan, 34
Mersenne (Marinus Mersennus), 120
Mitchell, Henry, 57, 58
Monk, Thelonious, 79, 82–83, 87
Morrison, Toni, 6
music: history of, 114–15; as mediator between genders, 113; philosophy of, 65–68, 89. *See also* African music; black music; blues; classical music; jazz; popular music; rap music; soul music; theomusicology
music history, 114–15
musical Platonism, 67
"My Black Mama," 130
My Bondage and My Freedom (Douglass), 53

Negro Renaissance: artists of, 16, 18, 91; white patrons of, 90–91
Nelson, Angela, 69
Nelson, Willie, 35
Nettl, Bruno, 36, 44
Neuman, Daniel, 114
Nketia, J. H. Kwabena, 35–36, 44, 46, 59
Northup, Solomon, 53

Odum, Howard, 26
"Oh Freedom," 54
Oliver, Paul, 109–10
The Ordering of Moses (Dett), 94

Partin, H. B., 51
Patton, Charlie, 61
The Peaceful Land (Still), 104–5, 106
Pearson, Helen, 115
Petesch, Donald, 3
Place, Marguerite, 97–98
Poem for Orchestra (Still), 105

Pollard, Alton B. III, 84, 86
popular music: philosophy of, 68–69; reconciled with religion, 71–88
Powell, Richard, 6
Primitive Culture (Taylor), 36
Prince, 79–80, 85–86
Proctor, Henry Hugh, 50–51, 52, 57
Psalm for the Living (Still), 101

rap music, 69, 88; criticism of, 80–81
Rawlins, Elliott, 76–77
Reagon, Bernice Johnson, 6
Redding, Otis, 78
Reed, Bruce, 21, 124
religion: importance of rhythm to, 21, 28–29, 32–33, 69–70; reconciled with popular music, 71–88. *See also* church; theomusicology
rhythm: African, 15–16, 22; centrality to African cultures, 6, 11–12; of black music, 21–23; impact of on black culture, 27–29; psychophysiological aspect of, 22, 25; and religion, 21, 28–29, 32–33, 69–70; as source of courage, 24–25
rhythm and blues, 78
ring-shout, 12–13, 19, 132
The Rise of the Gospel Blues (Harris), 5
Roberts, Hugh, 82, 87
Robertson, Carol, 40, 112–13, 115
Robeson, Paul, 92
Robison, Willard, 100
Royster, Philip, 69
Run-D.M.C., 79

Sacred Symphony: The Chanted Sermon of the Black Preacher (Spencer), 48–50
Sahdji (Still), 94
Schneider, Edgar, 4
Schoenberg, Arnold, 43–44, 95
Schopenhauer, Arthur, 38, 43
Schuller, Gunther, 114
Schwartz, Bernd, 71
Seashore, Carl, 22, 25–26, 29
self-reflexivity, 38–40; in ethnography, 40–41
"Sexual Healing," 85
Shaw, Artie, 100
Shelton, Robert, 35
slavery: spirituals as response to, 52–55
Smith, Bessie, xvii, 6, 109

Smith, J. T. "Funny Papa," 130–31
soul music, 83–85
Spand, Charlie, xvii, 62, 88, 107, 131
spirituals: and the blues, 57; correlation with black preaching, 47–48; critic's view of, 93–94; as influence on black composers, 16–17; as songs of liberation, 52–55
St. Helena Island, S.C., 12
Steckel, Clyde, 3, 64, 70, 118
Still, William Grant, 7, 15, 16–17, 29, 89, 92; critic's view of, 94; philosophical view of, 95–96; spiritual aspects of, 96–106
Stuckey, Sterling, 5–6, 19, 132
Sweet Honey in the Rock, 6

Take Six, 7
Taylor, Edward Burnett, 36
Temptations, 121
Theological Music: Introduction to Theomusicology (Spencer), 3, 5, 71
theomusicology: borrowing from other disciplines, 37–38; Christian, 107–8; descriptive, 71, 72, 73–81; as distinguished from other musicologies, 117–18; evolution of, 58–59; first premise of, 34–35; forum on, 49–40; normative, 71, 72, 81–88; predictive, 71; scholarly view of, 110; and study of black music, 36–37, 44–46, 50–59, 120; views of, 42–43
Thompson, Robert Farris, 6, 119; musical hermeneutic of, 30–32
Thorpe, Earl, E., 51–52
Thurman, Howard, 51
Tillich, Paul, 28, 32, 34–35, 38, 56, 86, 125

Tindley, Charles Albert, 75
trickster: association with ring-shout, 19, 132; black music-makers as, 20–21, 61; in black folk-heroic literature, 60
Trulear, Harold Dean, 72–73, 81, 86–87, 107–8
Tubman, Harriet, 7
Tucker, Sophie, 100
Turner, Victor, 20, 29
Turner, William C., Jr., 4–5, 48–50, 54, 122
Twelve Years a Slave (Northup), 53
2 Live Crew, 80

van der Leeuw, Gerardus, 13, 17, 19, 20, 24–25, 27, 29, 33, 38, 70, 90
Van Dyk, Johah, 127
Voorhees, Don, 100

Walker, Alice, 6
Walker, Margaret, 6
West, Cornel, 78, 117
Westfield, N. Lynne, 72–73, 81, 107–8
Wheatstraw, Peetie, xvii, 61
Whiteman, Paul, 100
Wilkins, Robert, 82
Will, George, 80–81
Williams, Martin, 83
Wilson, Nancy, 6
Wimberley, Richard, 85–86
Wimbush, Vincent, 56
The Winans, 7
Women and Music in Cross-Cultural Perspective (Koskoff), 111
Wonder, Stevie, 79, 86, 87
wringin' and twistin' (dance), 14

www.ingramcontent.com/pod-product-compliance
Lightning Source LLC
Chambersburg PA
CBHW030324080526
44584CB00012B/707